THE STARK APPROACH

THE STARK APPROACH

Reflections on Horses, Training and Eventing

IAN AND JENNY STARK
WITH TIM SMITH

MAINSTREAM
PUBLISHING

EDINBURGH AND LONDON

First published in Great Britain in 1998 by
MAINSTREAM PUBLISHING COMPANY (EDINBURGH) LTD
7 Albany Street
Edinburgh EH1 3UG

ISBN 1 84018 060 9

A catalogue record for this book is available from the British Library

Typeset in 12 on 15½pt VanDijck
Printed and bound in Great Britain by Butler & Tanner Ltd, Frome

Contents

Acknowledgements

There are many people to thank in connection with this book including all those who so willingly gave up their time for interviews and answered the many delving questions they were asked. It just isn't possible to name them all.

The many people who have provided photographs also deserve a big thank you. Whenever possible the photographs have been duly credited but in some instances it has not been possible to trace copyright owners and it is hoped that any such omission will be excused. Tim Smith is grateful to all those who agreed to be honest and constructive in their early thoughts on his effort. Thanks also to Seven Seas Ltd for the encouragement with the project and the British Horse Trials Association for the event records.

We thank John Beaton, our editor, and the team at Mainstream for their understanding, patience, encouragement and for taking on the original idea.

The Cast

Key Players
Ian Stark born 22.2.54
Jenny Stark born 24.3.54
Stephanie Stark born 3.6.80
Tim Stark born 8.8.81

Ian's Horses
Oxford Blue – Robbie
Sir Wattie – Wattie
Charlie Brown IV – Charlie
Clan Royal – Victor
Glenburnie – Glen
Murphy Himself – Murphy
Caliber
Stanwick Ghost – Jack
Mr Mackinnon – Duncan
Forest Glen – Glen
Sir Marcus – Marcus
Arakai – Harry
The Moose – Moose
Jaybee

Stephanie's Horses
Go Bust – Buster
Lord Patrick – Patrick

Dewpond – Sally
Douce Davie – Davie

The Owners
Dame Jean Maxwell-Scott
Mrs Susan Luczyc-Wyhowska
David and Alix Stevenson
Lord and Lady Vestey
Lady Hartington

The Trainers
Barbara Slane Fleming
Lars Sederholm
Ferdi Eilberg

The Grooms
Claire Colebrook (née Davies)
Caroline Powell (née Turner)
Ruth Day
Sharon Kitson
Vicky Welton

Introduction

L ife at the top of any sport is never easy, and having climbed to the pinnacle it takes hard work, guts, determination and more than a touch of luck to stay there. In the sport of horse trials today there are few still competing at top level who can claim to be more experienced than Ian Stark, a veteran of countless Badmintons, Burghleys, European and World Championships.

As a member of so many British teams, horses have taken Ian and his wife Jenny all over the world, since the Los Angeles Olympics in 1984 with Oxford Blue when the team brought home a silver medal and Ian finished ninth individually. Both Ian and Jenny agree that on the sporting front 1984 was the year that changed their lives forever.

Finishing third and sixth at Badminton with Oxford Blue and Sir Wattie propelled Ian into the spotlight and this success brought with it a sponsor in the form of The Edinburgh Woollen Mill and David Stevenson. This was a partnership which lasted more than eight years and gave the Starks much needed security from which Ian could develop his eventing career having made the brave decision to give up his work at the local DHSS office.

On so many occasions success breeds more success and as Ian cemented his relationship with both Oxford Blue and Sir Wattie, so the wins gradually followed. Nineteen eighty-five saw Oxford Blue continue his form while Sir Wattie required a year off with a bruised tendon sheath. But it was the following year that Wattie, Ian's favourite horse, came into his own when winning Badminton and then a year later formed part of the silver medal winning European Championships team in Luhmuhlen, Germany.

Nineteen eighty-eight was really the year that put Ian in the record books when he finished first and second at Badminton with Sir Wattie and the young

Glenburnie. Wattie in his gallant manner also claimed individual and team silvers at the Seoul Olympics during that same year. By now Oxford Blue was busy in the hunting field and the two bays who had taken Ian to so many great achievements were making way for a second phase of success with the grey boys, Glenburnie and Murphy Himself.

For three successive years Ian was to ride the two hard-pulling greys across the famous turf of Badminton Park. Nineteen eighty-nine was the year Ian first rode Murphy at Badminton where he finished fifth just behind his stablemate, Glenburnie. More medals came their way in 1990 when Ian and Murphy were part of the team at the World Championships in Stockholm. At this stage in his career it seemed to Ian that he was destined forever to take home the silver; gold medals eluding him at the major championships. By now Murphy and Glen were known throughout the world, their colour and strength on the cross-country capturing the hearts of the horse trials world.

Badminton 1991 gave the Stark entourage continued reason to smile when Murphy finished runner-up and Glenburnie came home sixth. Yet again, it was not Murphy's turn to take the winner's podium, after a fence down in the show-jumping saw them lose out on first place to Rodney Powell on The Irishman. That same year put an end to Ian finishing in second position when along with Glenburnie he captured the European Championships at Punchestown in Ireland.

After so many successful years it was inevitable there would be some lean times and when in 1992 Murphy was spun at the final horse inspection at the Barcelona Olympics it was a sad day for all concerned. Nineteen ninety-three to 1995 saw good results for Ian both at home and abroad as a new wave of talent started to make their mark in the form of Mr Mackinnon and Stanwick Ghost to leave Ian 11th and tenth in the world rankings. But Ian had to wait until 1996 for his first major three-day event win in five years when he took the honours at Bramham with Forest Glen. A happy hunting ground for Ian over the years, he had made a habit of winning the north's major three-day event at the start of his career in the early 1980s.

Nineteen ninety-six was a 'nearly but not quite' year for Ian. In the lead at Badminton after the cross-country on Stanwick Ghost he finished sixth with two show-jumps down. However, another Olympics beckoned, this time in Atlanta when sadly Ian suffered one of his rare falls across country. At the end of the season Forest Glen again rose to the occasion by finishing eighth at

Burghley, before being sold to America and there was optimism again in the Stark camp with two new horses, Arakai and The Moose.

The spring season started well with both Stanwick Ghost and Arakai taking everything in their stride in the build-up to Badminton. In the lead again on Stanwick Ghost going into the show-jumping, a disastrous five fences fell to leave them in 13th position. Despite this great disappointment there was much to be positive about after Arakai's solid effort claimed 14th position at the end of a hugely emotional event.

After the summer events were out of the way, Ian turned his attention to Blenheim and the Open European Championships at Burghley. Desperate for a change of luck after another crashing fall at Blair Castle on Mr Mackinnon, the whole team was delighted when a consistent Moose finished fifth at Blenheim, performing one of the few clear show-jumping rounds. More success followed at Burghley when a remarkably mature Arakai helped the British team to capture team gold. His cross-country round was simply outstanding and put paid to any talk that the horse was not experienced enough for such a challenge.

Ian and Jenny Stark live life at a frantic pace with many hours spent on the road travelling to and from events at home and abroad. Living in the Scottish Borders at Ashkirk near Galashiels has led to endless early mornings throughout the season to get to events on time. The Starks recognised soon after Ian gave up his office job in order to event full time that travelling south from Haughhead for every event would take its toll on horses, rider and back-up team. And it was with this in mind that Ian started to look for a base in the south for the spring season. Mentioning this to Henrietta Knight, who was then Chairman of the British selectors, she suggested that her brother-in-law and sister Lord and Lady Vestey might be interested in allowing them to stay at Stowell Park near Cheltenham. From this a relationship has grown which has seen the Vesteys become not only one of Ian's most longstanding owners but also firm friends. Every spring since 1987 with the lorry full to bursting point they have travelled south to the Vesteys where they base themselves until after Badminton.

Much of Ian and Jenny's time is spent attending events and functions for the many firms that support the team both financially and by providing products and equipment for Ian and the horses. At times it can still be a struggle to fit in the riding and Ian admits to getting quite annoyed when teaching takes him away from home and he returns to find the horses are not going as well as he would like. He remains fiercely competitive and still loves the eventing scene which has taken him across many continents and made him a household name.

Once Badminton is over the whole team packs up and returns home to the Scottish Borders from where they compete for the rest of the season. The yard at Haughhead has changed over the years depending on the number of horses Ian had to compete but, like many top riders, he always finds that if there are stables available these will gradually become filled. With this in mind Ian had four stables taken down to leave them with ten in their neat, compact yard near to the house.

For 1997 the stables housed Ian's five top rides and three horses for Stephanie who was aiming for a place on the Junior British team, an ambition she had fulfilled the previous year when the team took gold at Blair Castle Horse Trials. After so many years at the top Ian had decided he didn't want a huge string of horses again for the season preferring instead to concentrate on five rides for the year.

Their ten acre small holding is also home to some Jacob sheep which keep the grass down when the Starks are based at Stowell Park, while the house is guarded by Lottie the Rhodesian Ridgeback and Noodles the black and tan Jack Russell. Their location allows them open access to miles and miles of scenic rides and both Ian and Jenny could not wish for better neighbours who allow them to use their land for the many hours of fitness work in the early months of the year.

Ian's eventing career has always been a family affair with Jenny playing a crucial part as wife, mother, cook, groom and fittening expert all rolled into one. Well known for liking his bed, Ian leaves the running of the yard to Jenny and over the years groom after groom has said: 'Ian will plait, groom, pull manes and tails but there is one thing he very rarely does – muck out.'

Daughter Stephanie is now a keen event rider while son Tim takes care of the maintenance jobs around the yard when he is home from school, but prefers motorbikes to horses. The yard at Haughhead has seen a succession of top horses over the years and the names of some of the most famous remain on the doors. During any season there is a constant flow of new faces visiting the Stark household for tuition, hoping to follow in Ian's footsteps. People come and go during the summer months and it can be extremely busy with pupils and horses all benefitting from Ian's knowledge and experience.

As this book is being written Ian is preparing for the 1998 season and amongst the newcomers is the New Zealand thoroughbred Jaybee owned by Lady Hartington. Ian had competed successfully on him at the 1997 Auckland three-star event and everyone at Haughhead is very excited about his arrival.

Ian and Glenburnie, winners of the 1984 Scottish Championships at Thirlestane
(Claire Davies)

1

Ian Stark – The Competitive Edge

'I remember seeing Lucinda Green, then Prior-Palmer, walking about after winning Badminton. She was wearing a denim jacket and carrying a bottle of champagne. I wondered what she was feeling. I had always admired her as a rider, but I wanted to be her then, to be in her position, to have won Badminton.'

IAN STARK

From a completely non-horsey family, Ian David Stark's formative years were spent in Galashiels where he attended the local Galashiels Academy. At school Ian did nothing in the way of homework and was forever having time off, going to competitions and horse sales when he should have been at school. A chance ride at the local stables at the age of ten, when his sister Linda decided not to go, was the start of many achievements and he was probably one of the latest starters to pony club activities when he joined aged 17.

From his one lesson at the riding school, Ian became hooked and would spend all his spare time at Will Boyle's stables at Ladhope where he took every opportunity to ride whatever ponies were available. Bitten by the bug he left his sister and brother Derek standing when it came to developing his equestrian skills. Ian's mother Pearl has never been particularly brave around horses but when Ian showed a keen interest in riding she rarely tried to curb his enthusiasm. By the time he was 13, Ian was hunting fairly regularly and riding a variety of horses and ponies for a number of different people.

Says Ian: 'When Will Boyle closed the riding school he decided to concentrate on liveries and dealing. He brought in horses from Ireland and we would quickly break them, pull their manes and tails and trim them up before they were sold. I learnt so much, especially how to stay on board. From the early days when I first started riding for Will all I ever wanted to do was ride but when Stephanie and Tim arrived I felt I needed to make sure it would work before I took the plunge to concentrate on horses.'

Gradually Ian moved on to ride for a variety of people including his good friends Jackie Rodger and Bob Cranston. In 1979 a horse belonging to Ian and Jackie called Woodside Dreamer took him to his first CCI at Wylye and Ian was on his way. Deciding to work with horses full time, Ian was 28 before he gave up his job at the DHSS and said goodbye to his life behind a desk. His attendance record at the DHSS was no better than his school days and the flexi-time he worked became increasingly flexible.

In 1983 Ian finished first and third at Bramham on Sir Wattie and Oxford Blue. Then at his first international three-day event at Achselschwang in Germany in 1983, Ian took second and was a member of the winning team and the same year came seventh at Boekelo, the Dutch international three-day event, riding Oxford Blue.

Jumping into the spotlight in 1984 Ian finished third and sixth at Badminton before going on to win a team silver medal at the Los Angeles Olympics with Oxford Blue. A year later Ian and Oxford Blue formed part of the bronze medal winning team at the European Championships held at Burghley. Ian and Oxford Blue were lying in second place after a good dressage test and outstanding cross- country performance, when a brick out of the wall saw them slip to third place. Forming part of the team with Ginny Leng (née Holgate, now Elliot), Lucinda Green and Lorna Clarke, Ian also brought home a team gold medal.

Badminton 1985 was not so lucky for Ian when Oxford Blue had a nasty fall on the cross-country course and his other ride Lairdstown was eliminated. Lairdstown had previously been ridden by well-known Scottish rider Simon Rodgerson when Ian was offered the ride at Central Scotland to see if he liked him.

A change of fortune in 1986 saw Ian's first Badminton win with Sir Wattie and also a team gold medal at the World Championships in Gawler on Oxford Blue. In 1987 Ian was a member of the team that secured a gold medal at the 1987 European Championships in Luhmuhlen in Germany and he also took individual silver with Sir Wattie. Such outstanding success saw the British

A young Stanwick Ghost at Saumur

team parade at the Horse of the Year Show at Wembley. In 1987 Ian was awarded the Tony Collins Memorial Trophy as the British rider gaining the most points during the season when he secured 653 points. During the year Ian was placed 49 times, winning 16 times on ten different horses at all levels from novice to the European Championships.

1988 saw his famous first and second at Badminton winning with Sir Wattie, and taking the runner up spot with Glenburnie. Two silver medals were added at the Seoul Olympics and then in 1989 Glenburnie and Murphy Himself both claimed fourth and fifth at another excellent Badminton. Later the same year Glenburnie helped the British team gain a gold medal at the European Championships at Burghley and finished eighth individually.

At the top end of most major championships for more than 13 years, Ian is hugely respected and admired for his will to win and natural talent. Apart from that momentous Badminton in 1984 with Sir Wattie and Oxford Blue he says 1988 was also very special. 'To finish first and second in the same year was quite incredible, winning the European Championship at Punchestown was very special, but Badminton 1988 was something else. I had been out to Saumur with Griffin the week before which didn't prove particularly morale boosting when we fell at the water three fences from home so the first and second places were a dream come true.'

In 1989 Ian was awarded the MBE for his sporting endeavours and Stephanie and Tim remember the trip to London very well. Stephanie was proud of her purple skirt and Tim not so proud of his grey, itchy trousers which drove him nearly insane throughout the day. When Jenny asked Stephanie what had impressed her the most she replied that it was the lack of cobwebs at Buckingham Palace, while Tim kept asking if Ian had been given a BMW which left Jenny in quiet despair at her two young children.

In March 1990 Ian made the headlines for a less enjoyable reason when he faced a three-month suspension following the disqualification of Foxy V from an event in Australia the previous October. The headlines ranged from 'Ban hits Stark's world chances' to 'Stark is foxed by positive dope test' and it was an upsetting time for all concerned. Ian was banned from competition for three months by the FEI (International Equestrian Federation) following a positive dope test on Foxy V after he had won the three-day event in Werribee, Australia. The tests showed the horse had twice the permitted

Point-to-pointing on The Edinburgh Woollen Mill's Randolph Place (Anne Grossick)

limit of the pain killing drug Phenylbutazone in its system but Ian was at a loss to know why such levels had shown up.

At the time Ian said: 'Foxy had one small dose of bute at the start of the competition in Australia because he seemed to be feeling some discomfort which was thought to be caused by the blacksmith bruising a foot. In no way was I trying to hide or mask any unsoundness in the horse. That dose should have been well out of the horse's system before he had a second one at the end of the cross-country.'

Ian did not rule out the possibility of the horse being knobbled but the suspension was a painful time for Ian and Jenny and at one stage it looked possible that he might have been forced to miss the World Equestrian Games at the end of July in Stockholm. After a lot of deliberation and following an appeal by the British Equestrian Federation, the FEI reduced the three-month ban, by dropping the suspension and fining Ian £3,000. Ian was thrilled with the outcome and could hardly believe the total ban had been lifted but he did face paying the large fine and sadly the whole incident had left him with a very bitter taste in his mouth. For a while he was quite disillusioned with the sport, wanting to clear his name and get on with the job of competing. The suspension lifted, Ian and Murphy went on to represent Britain at the World Equestrian Games at Stockholm.

With Murphy Himself, Ian took individual and team silver in Stockholm and then with the two grey boys still in top form they took second and sixth in 1991 at Badminton, the last year they would compete there together. After such a long wait Ian finally claimed individual gold when winning the European Championships at Punchestown on Glenburnie before entering 1992, which was by Ian's standards a lean 12 months.

Throughout his career Ian has had a very good relationship with the press, understanding it is easier and more productive to work with rather than against the many journalists in the equestrian world. In both 1988 and 1991 Ian was chosen as the British Equestrian Writers Association's Personality of the Year. In 1988 Ian commanded 70 per cent of the vote and the award was one of the highlights of a day which ended with Sir Wattie, being officially retired in front of the Christmas crowds at Olympia. Says Jenny: 'Ian feels you have to make an effort with the press, they are there to do a job and it is better to be articulate and to get on with them. It is all part of competing at the top level in any sport and we have always tried to avoid any conflict, preferring to have a positive relationship. The one drawback is that we receive many calls for interviews and would sometimes prefer it to be another rider but at the end of the day Ian realises riding and the sport are his job and the way we earn a living.'

At the end of 1992 with the retirement of both Murphy and Glenburnie Ian came to what he feels was a major crossroads in his competitive career. After having such sucessful horses as Oxford Blue and Sir Wattie at the start of his career the two greys had kept him in the spotlight, but the novices he had been busy producing to follow them didn't quite make the grade and he went back to the drawing board to search for future talent.

The sponsorship with The Edinburgh Woollen Mill had also come to an end and Ian was left to put his efforts into Clan Royal, Dear Hardy and Stanwick Ghost who were then a relatively young team of horses. At the time all three were very promising and showed some of the best potential Ian had ever had in the yard but none of them were Badminton rides for 1993 and Ian was left without a horse for the event. Since his first ride at Badminton in 1984 his record has been quite exceptional and from 1984 to 1991 he competed every year on two horses. The exception being 1987 when the event was cancelled. 1993 was the year that Ian failed to have a horse ready to take on the challenge of the great event and instead he spent time commentating for the BBC. Ian recalls: 'I did not enjoy the experience of being at Badminton without a ride and remember finding it very frustrating. I actually went home before the show-jumping on the Sunday as I felt I couldn't watch anymore'.

Fortunately, about the same time, Ian was busy preparing Randolph Place, a horse owned by The Edinburgh Woollen Mill, for some point-to-pointing which Jenny wasn't exactly keen for him to pursue. 'I went to watch Ian ride in the Men's Open race at the Jedforest Hunt point-to-point and my heart was in my mouth. It was his first ride in a point-to-point for ten years and I was very worried. David Stevenson's wife, Alix, owned Randolph Place. At the race he was favoured by many to win and was in a lovely stride after two circuits when Ian and the horse suddenly disappeared out of sight behind some cars and I realised they had slipped on the corner. Somehow Ian managed to climb back on, catch up with the field and take third place which was quite amazing.

'We had also planned to run the horse at Cheltenham in the Foxhunter Chase and as the day drew nearer Ian got paler and paler and at the time I wasn't much help as I had terrible pains in my back and spent most of the time resting. The atmosphere was amazing but Randolph Place didn't rise to the occasion and gave Ian a crashing fall on the second circuit. It seemed ages before the ambulance brought him in. The examinations and X-rays showed Ian hadn't broken anything but he was very battered and bruised and the next morning couldn't move at all. By then it was obvious I had slipped a disc so we were both invalids taking an enforced rest.'

Between 1993 and 1995 Ian and his team of younger horses maintained their form with good placings at all the major three-day events before he hit the jackpot again in 1996 with a win at Bramham Horse Trials.

Since jumping into the big league Ian has constantly tried to put something back into the sport and to use his sporting prowess to help a number of charities. One such fundraising effort was for the local hospital when they organised an open day at Haughhead. Recalls Ian: 'All our friends had mucked in to help with the preparations as it was quite a rush and at one point there were about 20 people all cleaning tack. This was wonderful and meant that all our equipment was clean for the following day when I took a lorry load of horses to a local team chase at Floors Castle.' On another occasion the yard hosted an open day to raise funds for the Head Injuries Trust for Scotland. It was a very successful day with a lot of people turning out. Murphy was the star turn jumping some enormous looking fences which really pleased the crowd. At the time there were plenty of horses in the yard to be admired and all were paraded, from advanced horses to the novices. Some of the youngsters were paraded in hand and with Ian being a stickler for good turnout it was quite amusing when one of the horses got himself covered in large green stains which his handler was unaware of, but everyone else's gaze was drawn to.

Being a part of so many teams Ian has also been involved in numerous fundraising antics to raise cash for the Olympics and other major championships. One of the most outrageous occasions was organised by Rosemary Barlow, the well-known fundraising figure and involved top riders taking part in a revue at a dinner in London. Says Jenny: 'This was yet another of Rosemary's very successful fundraising brainwaves and the cabaret side of things was dealt with by former international rider and eventing's self-styled jester Julian Seaman. He must have wondered what he was taking on when Ian got dressed up as Olivia Newton-John in a black top and skin-tight pink pants

Ian holding Arthur of Manor Farm shortly after breaking his arm at Charterhall

and a blonde curly wig. Mary Thomson (now King) had the somewhat unenviable task of playing the role of John Travolta and danced with Ian on stage. Ginny Leng, topped the bill with an excellent take off of Madonna and even had to auction her clothes at the end of the evening. Ian also sold his pink pants which were not his to sell but it was all in a good cause.'

Ian is often thought of as producing horses in pairs, from his early successes with Oxford Blue and Sir Wattie and later the two greys Murphy Himself and Glenburnie. This in fact is not strictly true, as often one of the pair would be off the road with injuries while the other kept Ian in the spotlight.

Sir Wattie, jointly owned by The Edinburgh Woollen Mill and Dame Jean Maxwell-Scott is Ian's all time favourite horse and still going strong in his retirement with National Hunt trainer Henrietta Knight. Says Ian: 'He was just a winner from start to finish. In 1988 before he won Badminton for a second time, he won all his one-day events and then followed this with a silver medal at the Seoul Olympics. He really was exceptional and always gave 110 per cent. There was no way he would ever have the scope or talent of Murphy or Glenburnie, but it was his desire to please that made him so successful.'

Over the years Ian has sustained his fair share of injuries through falls. At Burghley in 1987 millions of television viewers saw him fall with Yair at the Burghley Bridge. Astonishingly he remounted and finished the course but was taken to hospital later for checks. The remainder of Burghley was spent on crutches with minor damage to his knee and leg. But after two days at home in Scotland he was back in the saddle and then won an Open Intermediate section at Royal Deeside and was fifth at Chatsworth three weeks later on Bridge the Gap.

He says that one of his worst falls was at Charterhall Horse Trials in the late 1980s when he landed flat on his face and suffered whiplash to his neck and back. Everyone thought he had broken his back and he was rushed off to hospital in an ambulance. Competing in the Intermediate section when the accident happened on the cross-country, the horse never really took off at one of the fences with the result that it somersaulted and landed on Ian. 'I remember lying there wondering what had happened. It was typical that I had just had two wonderful rides at Badminton and a week later I had a fall that nearly brought my eventing career to a premature end.

'Charterhall looked as though it was going to be a really good event but maybe it was a bad sign when a horse stood on Jenny's mother's foot and pulled off a toe nail. And Jenny's sister Catriona was riding with her hand all bandaged to support a broken finger. A young horse I was riding at the time, Abbey Point, won his section and then Foxy V and Mix N' Match finished first and third. As I was in a position where it looked as though I would win I set off in determined mood on my fourth ride somewhat inappropriately called Set Sail.

'For some unknown reason just when it looked as if we were going well he took a plain fence by the roots and I had a very nasty fall. Fortunately I was wearing a stock which I am sure prevented me from breaking my neck when I hit the ground face first. Thanks to this and my body protector my injuries were limited to damaged discs and vertebra in my lower back and neck. I was back riding one month to the day and had my first ride still wearing my neck collar. It was a very frustrating time not being able to ride any of the horses but at least I was able to see them being worked in the school. My injuries meant I missed both Windsor and Bramham and a trip to Seattle in America where I had been invited to teach.

'After that we christened the event "Charterhell" and I went back two years later only to have another fall coming out of the same wood when I broke my wrist. It was the same Red Cross team which had picked me off the floor two years earlier.'

Another fall, this time at home, at the end of 1991 left Ian on crutches once again. While trying a young horse, he severely sprained the ligaments in his left leg. 'I was told the horse could jump out of gaol, but unfortunately I never got that far because it couldn't turn corners and we crashed through the manège fence and it fell with me into the garden.'

Taking the rough with the smooth Ian remembers vividly the Barcelona Olympics when Murphy Himself failed the final vet's inspection when in with a chance of winning the gold medal. 'It was hugely disappointing and so sad for Murphy to end his career in that way. I had decided after my cross-country round that I would retire him following Barcelona but it was a very distressing moment.' says Ian. 'Thankfully whenever anyone talks of Murphy they always remember him for taking strides out of combinations rather than for failing the vet at the Olympics.'

When not riding Ian likes to spend any spare time skiing whether it is on water or snow and he has also developed a taste for free-fall parachuting. 'In another life I would have loved to have competed in anything fast and daring,' laughs Ian. 'I love the thrill of parachute jumping which is actually quite odd as I'm terrified of heights, but when you leave the plane it is a wonderful adrenaline rush and I need a regular injection to keep me going.

'Eventing has to be fun but at times during the major events, for some riders there is a lot of pressure as the nerves start and you begin to wonder how things are going to go. After a three-day event I often feel a huge sense of anti-climax, almost to the point of depression as the adrenaline high comes to an end. It used to be the case that after a big championship no one spoke to me.'

Barbara Slane Fleming (seated, left) *watches Ian and Murphy Himself at a team training day at Badminton*

Because of his great love of speed and danger, cross-country is Ian's favourite phase of eventing but over the years he has come to enjoy the dressage more and more. During a major trial the night before the dressage, cross-country and show-jumping Ian will religiously go through the test and jumps in mental preparation. 'Always at a three-day event I sit down and go through the dressage test in my mind, feeling how each section should be ridden and the rhythm of the pace and the transitions. For the cross-country I imagine the fences coming one after another as I ride round the course, thinking about where time can be saved and how the course will ride as a whole from start to finish.'

When the pressure is on, Ian somehow manages to switch off completely and will go and sleep in the lorry for a couple of hours. He can sleep anywhere, which can be very useful at times, and one year at Luhmuhlen fell asleep for an hour and a half and nearly missed the show-jumping.

Well known amongst his connections for being incredibly superstitious Ian will only wear gloves when they have been dropped on the floor and stamped on, while he always puts his left boot on before his right and his right spur on before his left. He admits openly that he is not the world's greatest spectator at horse trials, much preferring to be on the front line competing.

Not regarded as the best of time keepers, probably because of his busy schedule, Ian has nearly missed the dressage on a number of occasions but one of the most embarrassing he believes came at Thirlestane Castle in 1989. 'We had a lot of people staying that year and had a big party during the event. In spite of it being our nearest event we managed to make a complete muddle of the dressage times on the Saturday and I was sitting having breakfast when I should have been doing my dressage. Jenny drove the lorry very fast while I rang the secretary to apologise. We did not even have the excuse that we lived far away. Jenny nearly crashed into a bus as we hurried to the event but luckily we did arrive safely in the end.'

Over the years Ian has become highly regarded for his ability to pass on his knowledge to pupils both privately and at clinics all over the world. He feels a key factor to success for any rider is training and is a keen advocate that young riders should get as much help and assistance as possible during their early days. Ian has received help from well-known dressage trainer Barbara Slane Fleming for many years and still values her opinions and ideas. More recently he has turned to Lars Sederholm, the much-respected trainer of so

Positive Rain and Ian about to part company at Bramham, 1997 (Liz Rhys-Jones)

many top riders, for help and advice with his show-jumping. 'Whatever level riders are competing at, everyone can benefit from having someone on the ground who can provide another view on the way the horse is going. It is very easy for someone sitting on board to think their horse is moving correctly or producing a good jump, but a few words from a trainer or someone who has come to know the horse and rider and the picture can alter drastically. In the early days with Sir Wattie there were so many times when I thought he was moving well and correctly but Barbara, in her own quiet way, would point out a few minor changes and his work improved again and again.'

Now a respected trainer in his own right and much in demand all over the world, Ian says: 'I am probably quite hard when I am teaching, but that is only because I get quite ambitious for my pupils. If I see talent in a horse and rider I shout at them – but if I feel they're getting somewhere and are working hard then I'm quite sympathetic.'

Every winter the Starks' home is besieged by young pony riders who visit for a week's intensive tuition and for the past few years he has been responsible for the progression of brother and sister Jamie and Sally Atkinson from Durham.

Says Sally: 'Jamie started with Ian first on the pony training courses and liked his way of teaching. He does yell but I need someone to motivate me and at events he always takes the time to help out which does give everyone more confidence. Ian is very good at putting across what he wants you to do in a way you understand and has certainly made me ride more boldly across country.'

It was Ian who put Barbara Slane Fleming in touch with Sally when she was looking for a young rider for one of her horses and this partnership has gone from strength to strength. 'At Blair for the Junior European Championships, Ian wrote out my cross-country times which was a real help as I didn't really have a clue.'

At Bramham Horse Trials in 1997 despite Ian suffering a crushing fall on his chance ride Positive Rain he nevertheless stayed to help Jamie who was in the lead in the Young Riders' National Championships after the cross-country. Says Jamie: 'When I first started to go to Ian for help I didn't have a great deal of interest in dressage but this has gradually developed. Even when he is very busy at major events he will always be around for advice and to walk the cross-country which is a great help. At Floors Castle in 1997 Ian won the

Open Intermediate on Positive Rain while both Sally, who was riding Barbara Slane Fleming's horse, and I won the Intermediates so it was a great day for everyone.'

Ian has strong views on sponsorship and is a firm believer that there are no shortcuts on the way to the top. 'It takes a long time and a lot of hard work to get to the top of any chosen sport and I feel that the times of major sponsorships are over. I had completed Badminton with two horses in 1984 before there was any sign of a sponsor and when The Edinburgh Woollen Mill took us on board it was a great relief and their assistance for over eight years was incredible.

'I now have some wonderful owners and supporters in Lord and Lady Vestey and Lady Hartington as well as Aerborn, Super Solvitax, 3M, Westgate, Pittards and Burgess who help to keep everything on the road. But no one should ever expect that because of success it is their right to have a sponsor.'

Life on the horse trials circuit is both busy and addictive. And with that life of constant ups and downs come both good and bad years, all of which Ian and Jenny have experienced. After so many successful years in the late 1980s and early 1990s, the past two years have proved more difficult for Ian. At the Atlanta Olympics in 1996 Ian rode the third of his charismatic greys, Stanwick Ghost who had returned to form after a long lay off with tendon problems. In the spring of that year 'Jack', as he is known at home, and Ian had finished sixth at Badminton after a first-class dressage and cross-country performance. But, with a third Badminton title in his sights, Ian lost the trophy right at the very end when Jack hit the last two show-jumps. Their placing however, attracted a great deal of attention and the Olympic selectors breathed a sigh of relief to see someone with Ian's undoubted experience of the 'big league' back to form with a top horse. Summer arrived and with it the sweltering heat of Atlanta. A first-rate dressage left the team on a high with Jack's test earning his best ever mark of 35.2 penalties.

Despite the heat the British discarded suggestions that riders should perform the dressage phase in shirtsleeves and Ian told the press, 'Frankly I did not notice the heat while riding.' His shirt could be seen to be soaked in perspiration after he took off the £600 swallowtail coat, specially designed in lightweight materials.

But the flying start for the flying Scot fell apart on the cross-country –

Mr Mackinnon and Stanwick Ghost in the snow at Haughhead

their troubles erupting when the trail-blazing pair suffered a fall at the 11th fence. The gallant grey stumbled over the edge of the bank out of the first water complex, then put a foot into the ditch on take-off over the following fence. Jack breasted the jump, throwing Ian heavily over the far side. Never one to be put off, Ian remounted swiftly after checking Jack was sound and carried on to complete. Three show-jumps down and time faults the following day left the team, who had all suffered disappointments throughout the event, in fifth place. However, 1996 was not all bad, with a win at Bramham and eighth place at Burghley on Forest Glen leaving Ian in 12th place in the top 100 rankings.

At the back end of the season two new rides arrived at Haughhead strengthening the team and making the prospects for 1997 very exciting. Ian's faithful owners, Lord and Lady Vestey and Lady Hartington both invested in potential superstars. Lady Hartington's new horse The Moose arrived from Ginny Rose's Lincolnshire yard, while the New Zealand thoroughbred, Arakai was bought from World Champion Vaughn Jefferis by the Vesteys.

Le Lion D'Angers, the prestigious French three-day event in October, was The Moose's aim for the season. Ian was delighted with their performance after Moose finished ninth, coming home just four seconds over the time on the cross-country. He had only completed Intermediate events in the run up to Le Lion D'Angers and at the time Ian admitted the horse was green, needing another year to gain strength. His placing had, however shown he was a horse with a lot of ability who just kept on trying and filled everyone with a great deal of excitement as a future Badminton horse.

At Boekelo in Holland Arakai showed he was a talented individual when coping well with the course and giving Ian much to think about for the 1997 season. Says Ian: 'When the two horses joined the team in 1996 it certainly boosted morale and reinforced the team we already had. Mr Mackinnon, owned by the Vesteys was out of action at the time and the new horses both showed exceptional talent.'

During the winter, Ian will often spend time abroad teaching or competing and in autumn 1997 he competed in the Adelaide and Auckland three-day events. Both Jenny and Ian very much enjoy the welcome change of scene.

2

Stars of the Stable

'Horses have been our life, they have taken us to some incredible places, given us many triumphs and many heartbreaks but without them what would we have done?'

JENNY STARK

When Ian first sprang to prominence in 1983 after his win at Bramham in Yorkshire many people believed he had come from nowhere, a northern upstart who had only just entered the sport. In fact, in his own quiet way he had been riding every spare minute and whenever finances allowed him to progress. As a boy he secured the ride on the late Margaret Cranston's good jumping pony Black Magic who won many prizes on the junior jumping circuit. But it was his time spent at Will Boyle's that saw him progress from showing raw talent to become an accomplished and disciplined horseman.

Early successes came on Indian Tonic, a little coloured horse who was more than capable of performing a good dressage test. At about this time he was also riding Greyfriars Lass and Greyfriars Bobby — two greys who provided the next step up the ladder. Competing in the north during the late '70s and early '80s, Jenny and Ian soon realised his talents were not being noticed. And in a bid to solve this problem they knew the resources would have to be found to allow them to travel south. Riding a good horse called Woodside Dreamer, Ian travelled to the Wylye CCI in 1979 and finished a creditable 11th. But further successes at that level were not to be when the talented mare was kicked by one of Jenny's Highland ponies. Determined to make his life with horses Ian was by now fed up with his role in local government and finally

Woodside Dreamer and Ian competing at Wylye 1979 (Marston Photographics)

decided to make the break in 1982, the same year both Sir Wattie and Oxford Blue arrived at Haughhead.

Over the years Ian has ridden a great variety of horses which have somehow found their way to Haughhead. 'Looking out for new talent can either be very exciting or very disappointing,' explains Ian. 'Most years we make a trip to the sales while other avenues have included contacting owners after we have seen a horse we like at an event. On many occasions people telephone to say they have another Murphy and we rush off to take a look only to be very disappointed. We once went off to see a horse which was described as having real four-star potential. When we arrived the owners were very enthusiastic about the horse and told us it had a lot of ability. What we actually found in the stable was a nice little cob, which was wonderful of its type but no good for eventing at top level.'

Ian is a rider who rarely covets other people's horses and believes himself very lucky to have ridden so many talented individuals over the years. From the early days he has produced most of his own horses, including his first two stars Oxford Blue and Sir Wattie. When Murphy Himself came from Ginny Leng in a swap for Griffin he was one of the first horses to arrive on the scene which Ian had not started as a youngster.

Glenburnie on whom Ian won the European Championships at Punchestown in Ireland came as a six-year-old. Ian had first seen the horse two years earlier when his owners, the Maitland-Carews from nearby Thirlestane Castle, sent him to Haughhead for some schooling. Stanwick Ghost arrived in the Starks' yard as a new horse bought by The Edinburgh Woollen Mill as a five-year-old having competed at a few small competitions.

Two of Ian's more recent acquisitions, the New Zealand thoroughbred Arakai and The Moose, a giant of a horse by Euphemism, had both been taken up the grades by other riders, with Arakai being the more experienced of the two. But Ian is always aware that it is never easy taking over from where one rider has finished. 'Arakai was quite uptight when he arrived and we spent a lot of time getting to know him and letting him settle in. At his first Badminton on the cross-country he was so brave he gave me a lot to look forward to but his dressage requires a very careful approach. Finding top class horses is never easy as everyone is looking for them and when I was younger I enjoyed producing all the horses from novice stages. Taking a horse up to four-star level is a long process and I don't have that much time left!'

While searching for an event horse Ian would nearly always prefer a thoroughbred ranging from 16.1 hands to 16.3 hands. He believes that they are usually tough and have the stamina required for top level three-day eventing, but in many cases he tries to be open minded and will often take on a horse if it has a small amount of Irish blood or pony background in its breeding. 'I prefer thoroughbreds if they are good enough and have a suitable temperament but we have had horses of all shapes and sizes in the yard. If I had gone to see Murphy as a novice I would probably have said "no" but Ginny was obviously right in her choice. Many of the horses have come to me by word of mouth but I must like them instantly and have a gut feeling about it,' says Ian.

Jenny is always on hand when Ian goes in search of a suitable horse as he values her opinions highly and says she is always willing to point out any faults the horse may have. Temperament is very important and they must be trainable to succeed. When Ian buys a youngster he says there is often not a great deal to go on but as long as the type is suitable and he feels they have the quality and strength to cope with the sport it is often as much as he is going to know.

By choice he would not have a horse which was part warmblood and he avoids at all cost anything which is part Cleveland Bay because they tend to be lacking in speed and stamina. Similarly he would not normally choose a black horse as he thinks they have a 'funny temperament'. What is important, is that a horse has that 'look at me' attitude so vital for the dressage phase and that both Ian and Jenny like the general look of the horse on first appearance.

During the days of the two grey boys, Murphy and Glenburnie, Ian believed Glen was the ideal type of horse to take eventing – bred to race he was a big, strong thoroughbred by Precipice Wood. His views haven't changed and he would still prefer thoroughbreds every time.

Ian feels that for a horse to be top class it must move well naturally and be capable of showing a good medium trot without much effort. He recognises that with correct training and schooling a horse's way of going can be significantly improved but the whole job is made so much easier if the horse is built in the correct manner and moves well from the start. 'Stanwick Ghost is a horse who moves very well and looks elegant and always catches the judge's eye. His colour is also a help and he is very correct in his way of going which is helped by the fact that compared to Murphy and Glen he is very trainable.'

For a horse to attract Ian's attention it has to have natural ability over a fence and try to clear the obstacles. Over the years Ian has had both good and bad jumpers – and now tries to buy horses that have neat, careful rather than extravagant techniques.

THE STARS
Oxford Blue

Oxford Blue arrived as a six-year-old having been bred in Aberdeenshire by Norah Machattie and Liz Davidson. He was by Cagirama, a good sire of hunters, point-to-pointers and show horses, out of Liz Davidson's thoroughbred mare, Blewbury Fair. Liz sold him as a three-year-old to Polly Lochore, a well-known producer of event horses, who had represented Great Britain and now runs the hugely successful Burgie Horse Trials.

A lightweight thoroughbred, he was known as Robbie and was more of a ladies' show hunter than a top-class event horse and was described by Jenny's mother as a 'horse with pipe cleaner legs'. He eventually came into Ian's hands after Liz Davidson decided to buy him back from Polly. At the time Oxford Blue had been put on the market and Liz felt the only way of watching his career progress and preventing him leaving the area was to take on the ownership.

Ian tried him at the Royal Highland Show where he was entered for the working hunter class. After a good round he finished sixth even though he didn't immediately strike Ian as an Olympic contender being very green and spooky. On the flat Ian was pleased with the result but caused much laughter when he asked the juniors jumping the practice fence if it could be lowered so he could have a jump. Jenny rushed over to put the fence, standing at nearly five foot, down but it was soon obvious to everyone that he wasn't the most athletic or bravest of horses. Throughout their career and especially at the beginning, Oxford Blue sometimes gave Ian the feeling they would never finish an event but he always managed to get round and was never eliminated.

Oxford Blue was the horse that brought Ian to the forefront and took him from novice eventing to the Olympics. The bond that developed between horse and rider took them to a third at Bramham in 1983, third at Badminton in 1984 and that same year a ninth individual place and team silver medal at the Los Angeles Olympics. A year later Oxford Blue and Ian were individual bronze medallists at the European Championships at Burghley and then in 1986 claimed 11th place at the World Championships in Australia before he was retired – not bad for a horse who could panic at the sight of a cross pole!

The thoroughbred in him soon rose to the top even though Ian felt he looked 'lightweight', and his glamorous good looks always went down well

Oxford Blue at Badminton 1985 - the year he fell in the Quarry (Hugo Czerny)

Wattie in fine style at Burghley, 1984 (Kit Houghton)

with everyone. Many may have felt that Oxford Blue was the most untalented of Ian's top rides but they had a world-class partnership. Ian remembers: 'He may not have been the most athletic, but he made up for this by being so honest and that was what got us through the finish. He would do everything to clear a fence and would twist into some incredible positions. His whole aim was always to get to the other side, his heart was so big, he was always the perfect gentleman and had such a good character.'

It was after the World Championships that, at the tender age of ten, he was retired from eventing. A horse who had never had much time off, he had started to get quite stiff in his shoulders and by ten had completed seven three-day events. As an 11-year-old hunter Ian chased him twice before he was hunted by Lady Vestey who had many successful days on him with the Beaufort. Aged 19 and while out grazing in the field he had a stifle injury. Although the vet said that with many hours of box rest the injury might mend, after much discussion the decision was made to have him put down.

Sir Wattie

Incredibly over at the knee, but an out and out trier, Sir Wattie would stand in the yard his legs shaking as Jenny saddled him up to start out on the slow road to fitness during the winter months. Owned by Dame Jean Maxwell-Scott and her great friend Susan Luczyc-Wyhowska, Wattie was bred out of their roan mare Rosie by a local stallion Bronze Hill who sired a number of useful animals.

Broken by Bill Hughes near Galashiels, Ian was first asked to ride Wattie as a four-year-old, but after growing an angleberry near the girth area he had to be given six months off until this was sorted out. On returning to Ian as a five-year-old he promptly bucked round the indoor riding school at Dryden trying to dislodge his pilot. In spite of this Ian now had the time to put a lot of effort into the horse to prepare him for his first events and he started to think the stable might have a potential superstar. Wattie never overcame his fear of tractors and during the many hours of slow work he could hear a tractor from miles away and the girls riding him always dreaded the occasions when one appeared round the corner.

Wattie was a horse who lived his life in draw reins, and Jenny was always sent out to do the slow work with gadgets intact to ensure her safety. And although on the whole he had a very level temperament there were many

In 1986 Sir Wattie gave Ian his first Badminton win (Equestrian Services Thorney)

times when he took delight in throwing a huge buck while out hacking, giving his jockey a rather hairy ride. On occasions this buck left his rider deposited on the floor before he quickly made his way back to Haughhead on his own. Very intelligent, Wattie knew most of the dressage tests and Ian took great care not to practice whole tests in the run up to an event.

A horse with a huge heart, Wattie remains special as he was Ian's first ride at Badminton and despite his small lapses into naughtiness he is still looked upon as a true stalwart. His mother hunted three times a fortnight, and he inherited her driving spirit and determination that saw him cross the finish line at so many events. Says Ian: 'He had great stamina and we believe his breeding included a quarter Welsh cob. Wattie was very intelligent and tough and was keen to look after himself. He was just one of the gutsiest horses I have ever had.' An out and out winner the good-looking bay won all his one-day events in the run up to Badminton in 1986 and 1988.

At the Los Angeles Olympics in 1984 he acted as Ian's reserve horse after the selectors chose Oxford Blue. But his turn did come four years later in Korea when they claimed both individual and team silver medals. He was second at the European Championships in Luhmuhlen in 1987 but Wattie's Olympic endeavours were to prove his swan song and he was sent to Henrietta Knight, Lady Vestey's sister, who employed him as a trainer's hack and then retired him to the role of yard mascot.

Says Ian: 'Wattie was retired along with Mark Todd's wonderful horse Charisma after Seoul. He had been such an outstanding partner and friend over the years and owed me nothing. I admired and respected him greatly and along with Jenny I felt there was no need to ask him any more questions. For me it was the end of an era with both Oxford Blue and Wattie retired and it was quite like starting again even though there were plenty of good horses about.'

Wattie was a horse who went through life with the attitude of a six-year-old, rising to every occasion and proving so reliable. Although Ian didn't think so on first inspection, he had great power and scope with twice the natural ability of his stable companion Oxford Blue. Ian only ever fell off Wattie once at home when he was a youngster and they never parted company at a competition which is an incredible achievement.

'He had an amazing heart and still means so much to everyone, particularly Jenny who did so much of his fittening work. A talent for bucking was his only real fault and this was always forgiven,' laughs Ian.

Charlie Brown IV

Owned by Mrs Rowena Whitson from Biggar, Charlie Brown IV was by the thoroughbred Zara Crackle out of a pony mare. Known at home as Charlie he was the horse to continue Ian's amazing run at Bramham when in 1984 the pair took the title.

He arrived on the scene as a five-year-old after Mrs Whitson, a great hunt supporter in her day, sent him to Ian for a few weeks' schooling following a fall out hunting. She had originally bought the horse with hunting in mind but after he became rather headstrong she felt his manners needed improving before taking him out with the Duke of Buccleuch Hunt. Mrs Whitson was so keen to hunt with the Buccleuch that she thought nothing of driving the 100-mile round trip every week and following his time at Haughhead, Mrs Whitson decided to take Charlie Brown out hunting. Recalls Ian: 'The horse didn't take a great deal of time to sort out and when Mrs Whitson asked if he

Charlie Brown at Saumur, 1989 (Les Garennes)

was ready to hunt I agreed on the understanding that she took her time with him and didn't go too fast.

'The day started well and I remember Mrs Whitson suddenly galloping past and shouting about what a marvellous job I had done before she rounded the corner and was away. Thinking that everything was going well a few seconds later I came across Mrs Whitson deposited on the floor with broken ribs and a punctured lung while Charlie Brown galloped off into the distance. Needless to say she ended up in hospital and the horse came back to Haughhead for further training.'

Both Jenny and Ian have fond memories of Charlie and of Mrs Whitson who arrived at events wearing her lucky straw hat, often covered with a plastic bag on rainy days. Their win at Bramham introduced the Starks to pink champagne when a delighted owner emerged full of triumph and ready to celebrate.

After the early experiences out hunting, Ian took Charlie to Tranwell Team Chase where they were promptly eliminated. But the following week after a great deal of effort they won at Fenton, giving Ian some hope that the horse would go on to greater achievements. Says Jenny: 'We were never sure how Charlie was going to perform and after some events Ian would send me off to see Mrs Whitson to tell her the horse was nearly at his limit. But somehow he just kept on winning. At Bramham in 1984 Ian had said this would be the horse's last event but I had heard this so often I never knew what to expect. In the end they won Bramham with seven show-jumps in hand after leading the dressage and then finishing the cross-country inside the time.'

Charlie was a horse who often gave Ian a fright by banking his fences which happened both at Locko Park and Burghley much to his rider's discomfort. In 1986 they finished 20th at Luhmuhlen CCI after a fall in the show-jumping and they then went on to Burghley later in the year with the aim of Badminton the following spring. Says Ian: 'At Burghley we fell at the top of the Dairy Mound Steps and when Badminton was cancelled in 1987 I think Jenny breathed a huge sigh of relief as she didn't really feel Charlie was a Badminton horse and had been rather concerned about what could happen.'

In 1990 Charlie was sixth at Gatcombe before Ian took him to Burghley. This event was to be Charlie's final outing after a successful career which had surprised Ian somewhat from his early views when the horse first arrived in the yard. On his retirement Charlie returned to Mrs Whitson where he enjoyed a happy time before he passed away peacefully in the field.

Clan Royal

A favourite with Ruth Day, Lady Vestey's head girl, Clan Royal was bought locally by Ian and Jenny who in the early stages weren't sure if he was big enough. By Lord Nelson out of Miss Venture he rapidly developed and in fact grew to be a tall, leggy horse, with a neurotic character, who became known as Victor in the stable.

Clan Royal was the first horse Lord and Lady Vestey bought for Ian to ride after so many years of offering Stowell Park as a southern base for the team. He entered the fray at Haughhead as a four-year-old during Ian's extremely busy period when he had 14 horses to compete and often went round the school with his head stuck in the air, not wanting to come into an outline or do more than was necessary.

Bred in Dumfriesshire he was sold by his breeder as a weaned foal and then spent short periods of time with several owners as a four-year-old before a dealer in nearby Galashiels bought him. The dealer rang Ian to say he had a nice horse he thought would event and Ian decided that as the horse was so near he would go and see him. On first inspection both Ian and Jenny liked Clan Royal generally but thought he didn't move that well and he wasn't much over 16 hands. Ian felt the horse was worth a chance and took him home where he was turned out on the hill in the hope he would mature.

Says Ian: 'I bought Clan Royal just before we went off to the Olympics in Korea. When we returned we couldn't believe the transformation, he had grown incredibly and as he came floating across the hill I wondered if it was the same horse. By the time he was seven the chunky little horse I had bought was extremely tall and lanky and I was faced with the difficulty of connecting his front and back end as he was at this stage quite long.

'Dressage always proved to be quite difficult for Clan Royal and we found the best way forward was to do a lot of lungeing with him to strengthen his back and keep him relaxed for when I wanted to ride. He had quite a hot-headed temperament and we had to be very careful how we asked him to do things, coaxing and asking rather than pushing. His main attribute was his ability across country – he was a joy to ride in this phase – very quick and careful and he never got to the stage where he started to pull.

'As a novice we took Clan Royal to Holker Hall Novice three-day event. We were lying second after the dressage and I set off hoping I was going to have

Clan Royal and Ian competing at Blair Castle 1995 (Nick Morris)

a good ride. The course did ask quite a lot of questions but I felt he was ready for the challenge. Going well, we suddenly had a fall at the Stockade fence and Clan Royal headed off across the course. Jenny got a lift with Andy Griffiths in his car and arrived to find me muttering that it was one of the stupidest falls I had ever had. I got back on him and completed the course before an ambulance took me to hospital for X-rays on my neck, shoulder and back. Everything was all right and the horse show-jumped clear the next day despite the fact I couldn't turn my head to the left and kept insisting I was absolutely fine.'

Ian found Clan Royal quite difficult in the show-jumping and for a while jumped him in a hackamore. This often left the horse being quite onward bound in front of fences but as long as they stayed up Ian wasn't too concerned. At Thirlestane in 1993 Victor injured a tendon and this gave the horse time to finally mature and finish growing. He was placed at both Windsor and Punchestown and gradually rose through the ranks going to advanced.

'After Ian's disastrous round at Badminton in 1992 when he fell with Glenburnie it was great to go to Windsor with Clan Royal and finish fifth. It was a wonderful tonic for everyone and came at just the right time. We had put a lot of work into Clan Royal and let him mature slowly and although he never went on to do a four-star event we had a lot of fun with him,' recalls Jenny.

Glenburnie

A horse who continually injured himself and was notoriously clumsy, Glenburnie will forever be remembered as one of Ian's great greys, his eventing career running alongside Murphy Himself. Bred to win the Cheltenham Gold Cup, he was owned by Bunny and Rozzi Maitland-Carew of Thirlestane Castle, before he was bought by The Edinburgh Woollen Mill to run under their name.

Glenburnie started off being Rozzi Maitland-Carew's hunter. But his breeding, by Precipice Wood who won the Ascot Gold Cup out of a thoroughbred mare called Maytime, was to enable him to have the speed and stamina to conquer so much more. He was sent to Haughhead as a four-year-old for training. At the time, Ian felt he was very talented and would make a top class event horse even though his movement, and especially his trot would need a lot of work. A horse who took great delight in getting as dirty as possible the many grooms who looked after him during his competition days often resorted to baby powder to hide the green stains he acquired with great ease.

Ian tried to buy the horse but his owners decided they wanted to keep him and it wasn't until two years later that Glenburnie, as a six-year-old, started to be evented from Haughhead. For many years Ian believed Glenburnie was the ideal type of event horse full of power and speed, and with real scope.

Always difficult in the dressage, he spent many months off the road due to injury. In 1985 Glenburnie captured the Scottish Novice Championships at Thirlestane and finished runner-up in the British equivalent before taking 11th place at Bramham, his first three-day event. His excitable nature and tendency to damage his legs led to Ian replacing the horse's boots as soon as they had finished the dressage in a bid to keep him sound. Says Ian: 'I had quite a shock at Thirlestane in the Novice Championships. Glen was so used to hacking round the estate as a youngster that during the cross-country we had jumped into a double combination when all of a sudden he veered left. This was the route he was used to taking during his exercise and I had everything to do to keep him straight to jump the second element.'

The following year he took fourth place at Burghley and was noticed by the selectors. But immediately after the great event it was decided Glenburnie required a hobday operation which Ian found quite distressing – particularly as he ended up helping in the operating theatre!

A first at Brigstock in the spring of 1987, and the powerful grey appeared to be back to form and he was shortlisted for the European Championships at Luhmuhlen only for a leg injury to put him out of action for the rest of the season. Second at Badminton in 1988 he later injured himself during team training for the Seoul Olympics. But in 1989 Glenburnie started to come into his own, helping the British team to a gold medal at the European Championships at Burghley.

A good jumper but always difficult to soften in front of a fence because of his desire to pull Ian's arms out, the highlight of Glenburnie's career came at Punchestown in 1991 when the classy thoroughbred trounced the opposition to win individual and team gold medals at the European Championships. Says Ian: 'I worked incredibly hard on Glenburnie's dressage the day before his test to try and keep his attention switched on to the movements and not what was going on around him. I rode him, lunged him near a horse sale ring and polo

Glenburnie jumping down the hill at Gatcombe, 1989 (Liz Rhys-Jones)

field, both of which were in progress just to get him to relax and listen. And the next day he came out and did the most wonderful test to lie fourth. The speed and endurance phase at Punchestown was very imposing and a number of horses well in contention fell by the wayside. Glenburnie was very fit and pulled my arms out the whole way round. I will never forget that day or the next when he show-jumped clear and the gold medal was ours.'

Glenburnie was another of Ian's horses to take up hunting after their eventing days were over and it was a role in which he excelled. But in 1997 after time off with yet another leg injury, he was being brought back into work when he suffered a stroke. At the age of 19 he was buried at Thirlestane Castle near the dressage arenas and Ian reflected: 'I think he will best be remembered for winning the European Championships in 1991. He was such an exciting ride to watch across country, it is very sad that he has gone.'

Murphy Himself

Hugely talented but also hugely temperamental, Ian took over the ride on the volatile grey Murphy Himself from Ginny Leng. Murphy had already won Burghley with Ginny but he was becoming increasingly strong and after a crashing fall at the Ski Jump at Badminton in 1988 she decided to call it a day. With a badly damaged ankle and feeling extremely sore and shaken, she made the decision to part company with Murphy.

For some time he had been getting very strong and when Ian and Ginny discussed the idea of exchanging Murphy for Griffin it was an idea that had to be considered seriously. After lengthy talks it was decided the two parties would meet with their horses at Weston Park for a schooling session to see how they felt over some of the advanced fences. An initial run-out for Ginny and Griffin at a small fence made her ride in a much more determined way and the trial run continued without further hitch. The swap done and both riders happy, they left Weston Park with their new rides.

Both Murphy and Glenburnie never had many one-day outings in the run up to Badminton, Ian preferring to keep their routine fairly relaxed. It was always hard to believe that a horse like Murphy who could look so evil in the stable, trying to bite whoever walked past the door, was nevertheless a coward with other horses in the field often allowing them to bully him. While out at Phoebe Stewart's at Midlemburn one winter he let one of Ian's young horses, Sir Cabar, eat his tail leaving Ian quite lost for words.

A typical shot of Murphy (Liz Rhys-Jones)

Difficult to contain in the show-jumping the day after his cross-country, he remained a careful jumper and always tried hard to go clear, even if his great power sometimes ran them into trouble. One of the most powerful and daring event horses ever he was quite simply a law unto himself. Jenny remembers: 'I would spend hours leading Murphy out and riding Glenburnie and often stopped and realised I was miles away from anywhere with two very valuable horses, one being led. Luckily they were so good together and I never worried too much about losing one. For a horse with a headstrong reputation he always led very well and was happy doing that. I think Ian and Murphy did well together because Ian managed to get into his brain and work out what made him tick, but this isn't always possible.'

'Often on Murphy I felt like a pilot,' recalls Ian. 'There was little I could do to instruct him, it was more a case of balancing him and letting him get on with the job. One of his rare mistakes came at the World Equestrian Games at Stockholm when he hit the Double Oak fence quite hard. Everyone had told me Murphy would bounce the Road Crossing which was approached downhill. You dropped down one fence, then there was supposed to be one stride before the first rail on to the road. Murphy started to take charge and just ballooned the rails before the hedge. This was followed by the Double Oak, a maximum height parallel, which Murphy hit.

'I had thought he would back off himself and didn't really take any action to slow him down, but looking back I think he had lost his concentration at the Road Crossing.' A clear the next day in the show-jumping pulled Ian up from fourth to silver medal position, just outdone by Blyth Tait who took the gold for New Zealand.

Murphy's brakes always left a lot to be desired and Ian tried several different bits before he found an American cherry roller which seemed to suit him and at least gave Ian a chance of controlling his immense power.

'He was quite difficult to train and we never tried to dictate to him as there was no point. Most of his work was carried out either on the lunge or Jenny would lead him out while riding Glenburnie so there was as little fuss as possible and he was left to his own devices. In the dressage Murphy was always treated with great care to prevent him from exploding but while he was always the boss with humans, out in the field with the other horses he was a real wimp and would let them boss him about terribly,' says Ian.

Murphy and Glenburnie enjoying life at home in the mud

'He lived life on the edge, always just on the point of taking things too far before we had to readdress the balance. With Ginny he had won three three-day events before he came to me, and however hard we tried we just couldn't win a major event. At Badminton in 1991 when we finished runner-up to Rodney Powell and The Irishman, Murphy jumped through Centre Walk, taking just two strides instead of the more normal three or four, his power again winning against my strength. Both Murphy and Glenburnie were the most inspiring cross-country horses I'd ever had at that stage and they gave me so many breathtaking moments when I didn't know what was going to happen.'

Ian was pleased he had such a special horse as Murphy when taking part in a midnight puissance jumping competition while staying over at Stewart and Vivienne Christie's Busby Equitation Centre. Staying there for three of the Scottish autumn events Ian and the other riders took part in a 'fun' puissance in the indoor school. Ian couldn't believe it when the fence gradually rose to five feet six inches which Murphy cleared with ease to win and again demonstrated his enormous scope.

By the thoroughbred Royal Renown, Murphy was a horse who liked to be left on his own quite a lot. He always appeared much bigger than he actually was, standing 16.2 hands but often giving Ian the feeling he was a giant of a horse. Notorious for bouncing combinations, some of the most spectacular came at Stockholm in 1990 and at the bottom of the Beaufort Staircase at Badminton a year later. Ian found the best way to cope with such enormous scope and talent was to let Murphy sort everything out for himself. 'I knew Murphy wouldn't bury me into a fence as long as I let him get on with the job so that was always my policy. When I first had him I would sometimes try to dominate him but I quickly realised that this wasn't the right approach with him and after a few initial problems we won at Boekelo in 1988 before we fell at Belton when I tried to interfere with him. He always knew what he was doing and could either put in a huge stride to carry us over a fence or put in a short one to get us out of trouble. He was bright and intelligent but in many ways that was sometimes the problem because he was too intelligent. One of his pet hates was a whip and I would often set off with one at the start of the cross-country before deciding to drop it half way round as I needed both hands firmly on the reins to hold him. Murphy knew he was a star and could be difficult at times. I remember at a one-day event when I was bandaging one of his front legs, he suddenly kicked out, catching my ear with his back leg. You never knew what was going to happen or what mood he was in especially working him at home.

'One year I was working him in the run up to Badminton with Lady Vestey riding Glenburnie at Stowell Park. We started going at quite a pace and Murphy suddenly decided it was too quick for him and stopped abruptly before starting to walk. The next day he then ran away with me on the airstrip. It was such occasions that made riding him and working with him so special.'

At home whenever Murphy and Glenburnie were separated they would neigh to one another and pace the stables until their friend returned. When night stables were carried out Murphy was always the one horse in the yard to still be awake and alert. During the season he was given quite a lot of work but mainly hacking as he was already very finely tuned on the flat when he arrived at Haughhead and found going in the school somewhat boring.

Murphy and Glenburnie were retired together with Ian parading them at Burghley in the autumn of 1992. Still both fit and well they had given Ian everything and owed him nothing. After his retirement Murphy was often used to give pupils a pure dressage lesson in order to keep him active as Ian felt he would not enjoy being roughed off completely. He was kept quite busy with several appearances for charity including a dressage to music display in front of Princess Anne and came in very useful for lecture/demonstrations where he was able to show off to the crowd which he thoroughly enjoyed.

After his retirement Murphy also had a few days out with the Duke of Buccleuch Hunt ridden by the huntsman Trevor Adams. On New Year's day in 1993 they met in the square at Selkirk and Murphy was on his best behaviour only putting in one huge fly-leap. Once he realised the whip and hunting horn were for controlling the hounds he seemed to quite enjoy himself.

It was a heartbreaking moment when Phoebe Stewart rang to say Murphy had fractured his hock in the field and when Jenny took the call she was painfully aware that a dreadful moment in Ian's life had arrived. At the age of 15 and not even a year into his retirement Murphy was gone. He was a horse whose courage and determination had captured the hearts of so many and whose cross-country style made spectators gasp in awe.

Caliber

With his two greys retired Caliber a big, gentle horse filled the huge hole they left. He was one of the few horses to arrive at Haughhead already at Advanced level and fitted in well after Ian had retired both Murphy and Glenburnie. The younger horses in the yard hadn't quite made the grade and he took on the ride for Clive and Jane Storey from Yetholm near Kelso.

After Clive stopped riding Caliber he was passed to Caroline Powell (née Turner) who took the horse to Bramham and who later worked for Ian and Jenny. On arrival Ian soon struck up a partnership with this big horse who ran under the Super Solvitax sponsorship banner, and took him to both Burghley and Badminton. Says Ian: 'He wasn't what you would have called the ideal type of event horse as he was by a Hanoverian out of a thoroughbred mare. My first reaction was to say no when I was offered the ride, but in the end I felt there was nothing to lose and he stayed with us for two seasons. He went on to compete with Jamie Atkinson (one of my pupils) for a short time as a young riders' horse with reasonable success.'

A sweet horse, described by Jenny as 'shy and very gentle', he would hide behind his stable door with his eyes just peering over. She remembers the time Caliber managed to get cast in the stable and lay there waiting patiently until they managed to roll his huge body over. Renowned for being a poor eater, he never carried much weight and this was always a worry for Ian and Jenny.

Caliber was placed well up the order at both Burghley and Badminton, finishing 11th in 1994 at Burghley and tenth the following spring at Badminton. Despite his efforts he would not have been Ian's first choice of a four-star horse, but it was a position he filled extremely well.

Says Jenny: 'Out of choice Ian wouldn't buy a horse with Hanoverian blood and if other rides had been forthcoming Caliber might not have achieved the glory and success he was obviously capable of. Because of his breeding we had to get him very fit and lean and everyone would always comment on his appearance.'

Stanwick Ghost

Stanwick Ghost, the elegant grey with the wicked sense of humour came to Ian as a five-year-old. Known as Jack, for his 'Jack the lad' antics he is a great favourite with everyone. But Jenny feels he will probably go down in history as having lost them about £50,000 in prize money, as he slipped out of the top five at Badminton in both 1996 and 1997 when in the lead. Jenny and Ian fell for him the minute they saw his trot but nearly didn't buy him after seeing him show-jump. In an odd technique he threw his legs to the side but at that time Jenny thought he would improve and it was worth the risk. Jenny remarks: 'It is unbelievable how many times first impressions come back to haunt you!

'He can be quite grumpy in the stable maybe because he is permanently on a diet and in Atlanta he bit both Karen Dixon's groom and one of the show-jumping grooms. He is very deceptive and looks so soft and sweet but we quickly realised he was anything but sweet.

'One year at Brigstock Stephanie was lungeing him and turned round to talk to someone. When she looked back he had stopped and was staring at her as if to say "I'll only work if you pay attention". Everyone feels quite

Lady Hartington riding Stanwick Ghost at home

frustrated that we have him so highly trained and finely tuned but at major events he has been so unlucky and something has usually gone wrong. Out on the cross-country he has so much self-preservation but sadly this doesn't show itself in the show-jumping.

'As a youngster he qualified for the Burghley Young Event Horse final and at the last minute we decided to go. He was looking like a barrel as Ian had been busy with the other horses and after doing a nice dressage test he ran out at the first fence when the audience clapped and he ran side ways. The person who was judging the conformation didn't like him and Ian was very annoyed.

'When he started in novices he went up the grade very quickly because he always did such a flashy dressage test. When we bought him we were quite worried about his jumping but we were in the situation where we were desperately looking for a youngster and thought his jumping could be worked on. Ian said he was swinging his legs to the side over the fences but I just said that could be sorted out. It is often the case that what you see initially sticks with you. As a young horse he did well at Blair and was second at Saumur and fourth at Blenheim in 1993 before going to Badminton the following spring.'

By the thoroughbred Grey Ghost out of Stanwick Gold, Jack stands at 16.2 hands and was bought from Sally Williamson. Many think he is much smaller and has Connemara blood because of his naughty, pony face and his deep body and short legs but he has very good breeding, his mother winning a number of point-to-points during her career. Sharing the same grandfather as Sir Wattie, Ian feels Stanwick Ghost is the nearest horse he can compare him with.

'Stanwick Ghost is faster than Wattie ever was because he is a thoroughbred but both are very similar to ride across country allowing me to take tight lines over fences to save time. He is a wonderful horse on the flat and probably the most highly trained horse I have ever had. He is such a flashy mover that it would be easy just to rely on his looks!' Although he is a very laid back horse, Ian has found horses with extravagant movement can be careless show-jumping and he thinks Stanwick Ghost just finds that phase plain boring. When he was six he went from seven to 88 points and won the Scottish Novice Championships at Thirlestane as well as finishing fourth at Blair two-star.

Stanwick Ghost's first Badminton was in 1994 when he was eight years old. The event started well with a very good dressage mark which left them in third place but after a fall at the infamous Quarry Ian decided to retire. Jenny recalls: 'We took him to Badminton as an eight-year-old and Ian was very aware that people felt he had taken him there too young. With this in mind Ian set off on the cross-country riding more cautiously than he should have and had a fall at the Quarry. It is no good setting off in that frame of mind as it is always the type of course that needs attacking.'

Says Ian: 'Stanwick Ghost's dressage had shown he was now maturing in his way of going and had started to come up in front much more. He gave me a great ride on the steeplechase and in the ten-minute box he had the second best heart rate of the day which was pleasing as he's so greedy, and the only horse on the yard who isn't fed hay ad lib.

'We had him very lean and fit and started the cross-country well but he jumped into the Quarry so big that we landed at the bottom and he was rather surprised. I rode him strongly at the wall on the way out but he put down for another half stride and being green he caught the top of the wall and we rolled over. Somehow he was stuck against the wall but was not at all upset. I was the one who became upset when he started eating grass. Once we managed to get him up he was sound and fine but I decided to call it a day and leave Badminton for another year.'

In 1997 Jack put in a superb dressage display to lie at the top of the leader board. A magnificent clear on the cross-country followed only for Ian to drop from first to 13th after a disastrous show-jumping round when five fences fell leaving everyone feeling very low and quite aghast that this could happen to Ian two years in a row.

Mr Mackinnon

If it had been left to Ian to make the decision Mr Mackinnon (or Duncan as he is known at home) would never have entered the stables at Haughhead. When he went to see the horse with Jenny, Ian took one look over the stable door and dismissed him as a lightweight.

But Jenny had seen a certain quality in the bay 16.2 hand gelding by Southern Music and said Ian should take another look. It is believed he was found in a bog in Ireland and he was brought over by David Stevenson, of The Edinburgh Woollen Mill as part of a batch of six yearlings. Some of the youngsters were sold as three- and four-year-olds but Mr Mackinnon was proving difficult to break and throughout his career he remained cold-backed and would often put in a few good bucks after Ian was in the saddle.

He came to Ian as a five-year-old and was entered for Doncaster Sales as he wasn't ready to go into training, but Ian felt he wasn't looking strong enough or carrying enough condition so he stayed at home. Originally called Equorian Rhapsody by The Edinburgh Woollen Mill, after a range of clothing they produced, he was one of the few horses Ian decided had to have a change of names and became Mr Mackinnon. 'At the time Lord and Lady Vestey owned Clan Royal but he was injured at Thirlestane and I asked David Stevenson if he was interested in selling Mr Mackinnon who had now proved himself and the Vesteys agreed to buy him.

'After he had a few days off he was lunged before anyone sat on him. Even

Mr Mackinnon competing at Thirlestane 1995 (Nick Morris)

as a ten-year-old he remained difficult to get on at competitions and we would lunge him first. I was always conscious that he might be about to explode and go into his rodeo act as his back arched and I was in danger of finding myself on the ground. He would leap forward, rear, buck and plunge but I think it was simply because he was very naughty as a youngster. As a six-year-old at Eglinton I remember him going up in the air as I tried to put his bridle on. He careered off and when we eventually got him back he did it again. I decided to try a third time but suddenly one of Stephanie's horses who was tied up at the lorry panicked and pulled back leaving us with two horses running round the lorry park.

'When we eventually caught them I decided to put a lunge cavesson on him and when he went to take off again I grabbed the lunge line and he was so shocked he couldn't believe I was actually in control!'

A horse with 'a hell of a buck' Ian never lunged him with side reins, concerned he might pull himself over backwards. But, this difficult temperament was more than made up for by his elegant movement, which usually ensured a good dressage mark, and the enormous scope he showed over a fence. As a novice he rapidly rose through the grades and Ian was forced to take him slowly across country in a bid to slow down his rapid accumulation of points. At his first major event at Le Lion d'Angers he went extremely well, taking all the direct routes and coping well with two difficult water combinations and showing Ian how quick thinking he could be on the cross-country.

His most memorable placing was at Burghley in 1995 when he finished ninth and started to attract some attention as an eight-year-old. The selectors were more interested in him than Stanwick Ghost for Atlanta because he was the small thoroughbred type they were looking for but he succumbed to a dust allergy and then tweaked his tendon just before Badminton so all attention was focused on his grey stablemate. Out of action for a year, Mr Mackinnon was brought back into work in the spring of 1997 with a three-day event later in the season his aim. Sadly towards the end of the year he was found to have serious leg problems and Ian lost another of his talented team in an appalling run of bad luck.

Forest Glen

Forest Glen came into Ian's life after he had been ridden by Greg Watson. Owned by Jill and Bert Knight from Somerset, he brought Ian back into the spotlight when he won Bramham in 1996 and was one of the horses who ran under the backing of Super Solvitax. With Ian for two seasons he also finished eighth at Burghley before he was sold to the United States. The win at Bramham was Ian's first three-day event success for some years and the points accrued played a major part in Ian achieving fifth place in the world rankings for the season.

Sir Marcus

An uncomplicated horse, Sir Marcus has been very consistent for Ian. Allergic to flies and suffering from a dust allergy, Marcus flew up the grades with Ian, winning the young event horse class at Chantilly and finishing fourth overall, before he had a year off for a hobday operation. At Chantilly, Marcus, by State Diplomacy, survived a nasty moment at the water before galloping on to return the fastest time of the day. Owned by the Traves family from near Selby and also running under the Super Solvitax banner, both Ian and Jenny thought deep down that Marcus wasn't going to be a four-star horse but he was very reliable and always finished at the top end at most events.

Arakai

Produced in New Zealand by Gee Davison, Arakai was brought over to England by Vaughn Jefferis in the spring of 1996. A lithe, wiry horse, he is one of Jenny's favourites. Slightly anxious in the stable, sometimes it is difficult to get him to eat enough and not fret. By Ring the Bell, the sire of the 1997 Grand National winner Lord Gyllene, he has a sharp, slightly anxious temperament and worries about the dressage but on the cross-country his performances are inspirational and he is very genuine and bold.

A horse who likes a lot of company and doesn't enjoy being on his own much, Arakai gets very attached to whichever horse is in the stable next to him. Because of this and with the aim of keeping him relaxed and calm, Ian always tries to have a horse near him otherwise he can get quite excited which doesn't help him in the long run. Says Ian: 'Arakai is a horse that we try to turn out in the field as much as possible to keep him relaxed but we only turn

Forest Glen winning Bramham 1996 (Pleasure Prints)

Some current stars: (left to right) *Stanwick Ghost, Sir Marcus, Arakai, Mr Mackinnon, The Moose* (Expo Life)

him out in the field on his own with other horses in the fields nearby as I'm too worried about him getting kicked.'

Ian feels Arakai is one of the most athletic horses they have had in the yard and is full of hope for the future with him. Nimble and clever, he has a very natural jump, is sharp and there appears to be no end to his courage and enthusiasm for the job. Ridden across country in a snaffle, he is very different from Murphy and Glenburnie who were always such tiring rides.

Originally called Always Happy, Vaughn Jefferis didn't like the name and changed it to Arakai, calling him Happy in the stable but Ian took an instant dislike to that and changed his stable name to Harry. Arakai provided Ian with a lot of hope for the 1997 season and he soon became a favourite with the team.

The Moose

A huge horse, Moose likes to think he is the boss, towing people round on the end of the lead rope. A favourite with groom Vicky Welton and Tim Stark, Moose gives the outward impression of being incredibly cool. By Euphemism, he had won about 20 points when he was bought for Ian by Lady Hartington from Ginny Rose in Lincolnshire. A horse with a great desire to be in charge there were many occasions during his first full season with Ian in 1997 when he left grooms and helpers battered in his bid for the best grass in the field. A consistent year saw Moose end the season on a high note with a superb effort at Blenheim in the autumn.

3

Badminton – The Rough and the Smooth

'I help in the ten-minute box and at the steeplechase, and like getting involved but sometimes I know when to stand back and let everyone get on with it. It's stressful enough without a million people all rushing around like headless chickens.'

STEPHANIE STARK ON BADMINTON 1997

In 1986 Ian realised a life-long ambition when he brought home to Scotland the Whitbread Trophy after winning one of the eventing world's highest accolades at Badminton.

'Badminton 1986 was even more exciting than the Olympics,' recalls Ian. 'I was 32 at the time and to win was quite fantastic. I remember thinking the Olympics and World Championships are something which seem to just happen but winning at Badminton is every event riders' dream and it was a real highlight in my career.

'On the Friday I did both tests with Glenburnie and Wattie being first and last to go. Glenburnie was only eight at the time and did a very respectable test. Wattie was very excitable and I took him off for a hack to try and calm him down. When he finished in third and Glenburnie was tenth it was more than I could have hoped for.

'I walked the cross-country on the Friday evening and the ground had improved a lot after some rain but then it proceeded to rain throughout the night. When I looked at the course on the Saturday morning the ground was quite bad and I thought it would be better to withdraw Glenburnie and save him for another day. On the steeplechase with Wattie we incurred 0.8 of a time penalty, the going was so sticky and I didn't want to push him too much with the cross-country to come.

'There had been a lot of problems on the course and I was very pleased to hear a loud cheer and lots of support as we set off. On the first half we went really well and as we got more confident I just decided to let him keep going. At the Vicarage Vee I remember his back foot slipping into the ditch and he almost threw me out the front door. At the fence his tummy touched the ground and I thought that if I could get away with that then I could get away with anything.

'He went to jump and slipped but although he was tired he gave me a brilliant ride after that. I was quite concerned about the Lake and as we approached I was all over the place but Wattie being so good he just kept on going not taking any notice of me. After the effort at the Lake he was quite tired but he was such a trier and when we came through the finish to take the overnight lead the pressure soon turned to the show-jumping.

. 'Because of more rain overnight the organisers brought this phase forward. I thought Wattie would be exhausted but he took off with me at the trot-up and I was actually quite pleased by this behaviour. Last to go, I felt terrible. It was still raining and I didn't even realise we had hit the third fence, the other fences remained intact and we had won the title. Everyone was very excited and there was a lot of celebrating with a champagne reception at The Edinburgh Woollen Mill's base at Langholm on the way home to round everything off.'

The 1987 Badminton was cancelled because of torrential rain and 1988 was to prove a very special year for Ian when he competed on Sir Wattie and Glenburnie. At the beginning of the year Ian was quite worried that he may not have enough advanced horses to keep him going for the season but after his efforts that spring his worries ended. As soon as Ian arrived at Badminton he dashed off to London for a radio interview with John Dunn and the whole week continued in a flurry of excitement and energy.

As Wattie was unloaded from the lorry he knew exactly where he was and marched proudly into the stables and Glenburnie also appeared keen to be back. The horses had both been given a good work out at Stowell Park before setting off for Badminton with Alison Duthie on hand to groom. Having won in 1986 Ian was quite nervous about the 1988 running and admits his stomach started to churn even before he drove the lorry into the estate.

'On the morning of the competitors' briefing I managed to sleep in but by the time of the first veterinary inspection I had woken up and once both horses had successfully passed I could relax again,' says Ian. 'The trot-up is one of the worst parts of the event and always a relief when that is over and done with. Glenburnie had been drawn to do his dressage on the Thursday, which helped in trying to keep him settled, as there would be fewer people about. He was always a horse who became quite naughty in the dressage and if he had a large audience to play to he made the most of it by showing off.

'On the day of the dressage I gave him a lot of work early in the morning in the hope that I could just do about ten minutes before entering the arena. Some of my connections thought I had missed my time but I often come up to the arena at the last minute. Glenburnie was quite excited but he did a very good test and went into the lead at the end of the first day. As his preparation had gone so well I decided to do exactly the same with Wattie, taking him for a hack in the morning. He did another good test only jogging once during the walk movement and I could now start looking forward to the cross-country.

'We were lying second and fourth after the dressage and I knew we could do well in the cross-country, but I'd never dreamed of doing so well. I have always felt there is only one way to ride round Badminton and that is in a bold, positive manner attacking the fences. Glenburnie went extremely well and tried very hard, his relentless gallop taking us from one fence to the next. I had considered changing his bit but was glad in the end that I didn't as he would probably have pulled even harder. Climbing back on Wattie was quite a funny experience as he was so different to Glenburnie. There was a slightly hairy moment at the Lake but with his years of experience he knew just what to do to get us out of trouble.

'Both horses were fresh the following morning for the trot-up but were much quieter to handle than at the inspection on the Wednesday. I was very nervous beforehand and hadn't had time to walk the show-jumping course and was going on what I'd been told, so I kept imagining I would jump a wrong fence. The morning actually went very quickly as there seemed to be so much to do and when Glenburnie went clear that gave me a lot of confidence.

'There was silence as I came in on Wattie and a huge gasp from the stands as he touched a brick on the wall. But he was brilliant and I knew when we went into the show-jumping we were going to do well; he pricked his ears and responded to the atmosphere. There was so much pressure on, especially when it looked as if I could do the double, but after Wattie's round I just felt numb. I was so pleased for Glenburnie as well, I'd always had a lot of faith in him and thought he would be good, but until a horse goes round Badminton you never know how good it is.

'If anyone had told me I was going to be first and second in the January of that year I would have laughed and said it was impossible. Somehow everything just seemed to go right and the whole event went like a dream.' Ian's first and second at Badminton in 1988 made history and he was the first rider ever to fill the top two places.

Preparing for Badminton 1990 was its usual hive of activity with half a day spent in Carlisle parading Sir Wattie at the racecourse while Ian also took part in a Fell pony race for charity. David Stevenson, Gordon Richards and Frazer Hines from *Emmerdale Farm* were also taking part in the star-studded race and Ian knew the activity at Badminton a few days away would be very different.

Says Jenny: 'Our whole life swings from one Badminton until the next; other people might note the passing of another year by Christmas celebrations or the arrival of the New Year but for us it is from one Badminton to the next. In the spring of 1990 Ian fell with Glenburnie at Belton but fortunately this didn't appear to have put them off and both grey boys were looking extremely fit and well as the event approached where they finished 14th and 15th.

'The following year Ian finished second with Murphy and sixth on Glenburnie. He missed winning by a whisker after Murphy's strong, argumentative character led to a pole down in the show-jumping at one of the easiest fences. They held the lead after the cross-country which had been a superb round but Murphy was still full of life for the show-jumping. Glenburnie also hit one fence but we were delighted to have two horses in the top six. It was a great thrill when Ian paraded the two horses and the cheer that went up was quite the loudest I had ever heard.

'In 1992 Murphy was excused Badminton and it felt quite odd to have only Glenburnie there after taking both horses for the previous three years. There was a lot of pressure on Ian to win after he claimed the European Championships at Punchestown the year before and he was strongly tipped as the favourite. The six years since we had first taken Glenburnie to Badminton as a young horse had flown by and all of a sudden we had started to think about retiring him. In the end the event turned out to be something of a disaster when Ian and Glenburnie had a bad fall at the Ha-Ha which put them out of the competition to everyone's disappointment.

'In 1993 Ian didn't have a ride which made him difficult to live with and then the following year he had a fall with Stanwick Ghost at the Quarry so for a couple of years we had quite a testing time at Badminton after so much success. Thanks to Caliber, Ian finished tenth in 1995 before Stanwick Ghost recorded a sixth place in 1996.'

In second place after the dressage, Ian and Stanwick Ghost had opened their efforts with a wonderful high, earning ten from ground jury president Lord Carew as they came down the centre line to finish. The following day Ian and the flying grey took on the challenge of the cross-country at close of play. Coming home some 14 seconds inside the time to great cheers they managed to snatch the lead from David O'Connor and Custom Made to head the leader board after a thrilling round in which Stanwick Ghost lost a front shoe.

Going into the show-jumping Ian was all too well aware of the enormous task he faced to win the coveted Badminton title. The further they went the more hopeful the crowd became when, with just two fences to go, their grip on the trophy went. Stanwick Ghost dislodged the penultimate fence, an upright gate, and then hit the final fence. They finished in sixth place in the final reckoning.

The run-up to Badminton in 1997 was controversial from the outset after a deluge of entries led to balloting and a number of foreign riders were upset by the prospect of only taking one horse to the Mitsubishi Motors Championship. Ian was one of four British riders allowed to take two horses and this in itself had led to a great deal of discussion but he felt both Stanwick Ghost and Arakai deserved the run and their preparation up to the event had gone smoothly. Taking Moose to Compiegne in France the week before Badminton gave them both a chance to relax and not feel over pressured.

The weekend before Ian had taken Arakai to Goring Heath for the dressage and show-jumping after which he was rested for a couple of days. Says Ian: 'There is only so much preparation you can do before an event and it is so easy, especially in the days before Badminton to overdo the work.' While Ian was away the horses were kept ticking over with a couple of days off, some hacking and slow trotting to keep their minds focused but not too active.

It was a cold, blustery Wednesday that greeted Ian for the first inspection at Badminton in 1997. At 10 a.m. the competitors receive their first briefing

Ian and Stanwick Ghost with Lady Vestey (Tim Smith)

and this is followed by the inspection of the course with the trot-up at 4.30 p.m. The team had settled in the day before with Ruth Day looking after Arakai and Sharon Kitson taking care of Stanwick Ghost's needs.

Both Stephanie and Vicky drove in everyday after seeing to Go Bust and Marcus at Stowell Park who were aimed at Punchestown in Ireland just a few days after Badminton. The five days always bring a social whirl, and there are challenges and pressures unlike any other event. At the trot-up owners Lady Vestey and Lady Hartington watched nervously from the sidelines as both horses trotted-up well and confidently. Ian, sporting a bright yellow shirt, received a lot of comments from the other riders and crowds which all added to the occasion. Wednesday also provided Ian with the opportunity to walk the course on his own and take in his first impressions of some of the fences he would meet galloping round just two days later.

Thursday was an early start for Ian and Arakai and was another windy day.

Ian woke at the crack of dawn to work Arakai and settle him in preparation for his test before taking himself off to the lorry for some peace and quiet and to get his thoughts together before changing for the dressage. Ian admitted to feeling quite ill before the test but once on board he kept focused on the job.

Following Leslie Law into the arena after some quiet work with Barbara Slane Fleming, Ian had wished for more settled weather but after riding tests in some of the most extreme weather conditions over the years, he more than recognises everyone is in the lap of the gods. 'I tried to keep Arakai as relaxed as possible,' says Ian. 'He can get very tense and his best work at the spring events in the weeks before Badminton had always been when the arena was quiet and calm. He worked-in very well considering there were so many distractions and when one of the signs lifted up in front of us as we entered the arena I wasn't sure what was going to happen. Luckily he tolerated that and after a poor halt, he started to settle and produce some good work, coming up the centre line at the end very well. One of the flying changes was very good while the other left something to be desired, but I was still pleased.'

Ian's dressage mentor Barbara Slane Fleming was also pleased with the test, considering Arakai's inexperience, which left them on a score of 66 penalties. The media showed a great deal of interest in him throughout the event and once Ian had left the arena journalists pounced to find out more about the New Zealand import. At the end of the day the Swedish rider Linda Algotsson, a mathematics and biology teacher, shared the lead with the American David O'Connor.

Paddy Muir from Cleveland and Archie Brown, who had swapped placings at the top of the board with Ian and Stanwick Ghost throughout the spring season at various events, was in third. And once all the attention had died down Ruth took Arakai off for some grass and to let him settle out of the way in front of the house.

With Stanwick Ghost's test taking place at the end of the day on Friday, Ian and Mrs Slane Fleming used the Thursday to put in some work in an effort to make him more controllable, Ian describing him as 'quite wild'. After an hour and 45 minutes' work Ian was pleased with the result and after a rest set out on a cross-country walk for the second time with Jenny and Charlotte Ridley, who was also competing, and had asked for some advice. As is the ritual at Badminton, Thursday evening was the cocktail party at

Ian and Stanwick Ghost get to work (Tim Smith)

Badminton House, and a time to relax before the pressures really began to mount.

Another early start on the Friday morning saw Ian walking the course for a final time and giving Stanwick Ghost another work-out before his test at the end of the day. Taking the opportunity to work him hard and get him very much tuned in to his efforts, Ian wanted Stanwick Ghost to work stronger in his canter while at the same time keeping him calm. The weather had by now settled as the wind disappeared and everyone was pleased with proceedings so far. As this would be his last major session before the test, Ian finished off by taking him for a canter and then a walk in the park to take his mind off the intensity of the dressage.

A few hours later and things were very different with many anxious faces watching them both as they made final preparations before entering the arena. The atmosphere was electric, probably more so as Ian was the final competitor of the day to go at 4.52 p.m. and a lot was expected of them. As

Ian, Lady Hartington and Sharon Kitson (right) *after Stanwick Ghost's superb dressage test* (Tim Smith)

they set off on what was to be a truly superb test, the crowd held their breath and Stanwick Ghost came up with the goods to lead the first phase on a score of 46.2 penalties after a test which many felt had been rather harshly marked.

The score left little room for complacency and there were many more challenges to come. In second place stood Robert Lemieux on his great campaigner Just An Ace and in equal third place came Swedish rider Linda Algotsson on her 16-year-old Lafayett and American, David O'Connor on Custom Made. After hasty congratulations, Radio Badminton interviewed Ian about his test and he then gave Stanwick Ghost a quick jump over the practice fences before being whisked off to a press conference.

Cross-country day dawned and with it an early morning interview for Ian on Radio Badminton. 'I got out of bed at about 8 a.m. feeling very sick and had been awake for ages just thinking about getting on Arakai and setting off,' recalls Ian. 'It was agony waiting. I had begun to wonder how he would cope with the ground as the rain over night had made the conditions quite greasy and decided to put bigger studs in to try and stop him slipping. Many people thought I would use him as a practice round, but at major events such as Badminton, no round is a trial run and the course must always be treated with

Walking the course with Charlotte Ridley (Tim Smith)

the respect it deserves. As he is a good galloping horse, my intention was to try and keep up with the time.'

With phase A, the first section of the roads and tracks, successfully completed and the horse checked over by Ruth and Sharon, Ian embarked on the steeplechase. Arakai gave him a great ride and once Stephanie and Vicky had made sure everything was intact they set out on phase C, the second roads and tracks phase.

Everyone was pleased to see them heading towards the ten-minute box safe and sound and the back-up team took over while Ian collected his thoughts for phase D, the cross-country. Said Ian: 'I felt very sick before the start and wasn't quite sure what to think about. Arakai had been very good on the first three phases, he looked fit and well and I just wanted to get back on when the time was right.'

As one of the pathfinders on the course, there was much attention on Ian's round as riders watched the closed circuit television eager to see how the course was riding. There was a great cheer as they set off and even more delight as they finished, Ian with a broad smile on his face, having stuck to his plan and taken most of the direct routes in their stride without any major hiccups. Said Ian: 'Harry gave me a great ride, he is a horse with so much potential and we had no real problems at all, it was wonderful to have such a good first round.' With three-and-a-half hours to wait before he set out on Stanwick Ghost, Ian had plenty of time to think about his round and make any necessary changes to the route.

Having been round earlier in the day, Ian was one of just two riders in the end who had a second ride at Badminton 1997 – the other being Leslie Law. Stanwick Ghost gave Ian a strong ride on the steeplechase as the clouds were coming in again and the sky became overcast but during the afternoon the ground had dried and Ian was unconcerned about the conditions.

Before he set off, Ian's plan with Stanwick Ghost was also to go the long route at the Quarry if the time looked good as this would avoid what could be a very steep landing at the bottom of the slope. Ian and Stanwick Ghost were the only ones left who could overhaul David O'Connor's effort and there was a great deal of pressure on the team at this stage in the day.

As Ian and his magnificent grey set out on the cross-country there was a huge cheer and they were away with 31 fences to negotiate within the optimum time of 12 minutes and ten seconds. Jenny waited in the ten-minute box looking worried and listening to the commentary as one by one they successfully overcame the hurdles and obstacles put in their way. 'The Shogun Seat was the first fence and as usual I simply aimed to get over. I remember Lucinda Green saying she used to come to the first fence and leave the horse to sort it out, but I try very much to help the horse out here, so that his confidence will grow,' says Ian. 'There is also a downhill approach to the first fence which is a good solid jump so there is no room for complacency. Both Harry and Jack set off well so there was no cause for concern at this stage.

'The Parallel Rails at two were a new fence for 1997 and I tried to open the horses up a little towards the second fence. This year the spread was quite wide with a sloping approach but it was built from good solid timber. A narrow looking fence, the wagons at either side made it appear even narrower and you needed a bit of pace coming into it to make the spread. Jack slightly pecked on the approach to this fence and nearly landed on his head but he managed to pick himself up, jump the fence and carry on.

'The Save the Children Fund complex – fences three, four and five – were the first combination on the course with big log piles at three and four with the Ha Ha in the middle. In 1992 I tried to jump the Ha Ha in one go with Glenburnie but we ended up in a heap on the floor and I've given it more respect ever since. It is always important here to look for a good line through the whole complex, pop down the hole, ride for one stride and then push out on a forward-riding four strides. I remember in 1995 holding to the final log pile out and then burying Caliber in the bottom before he made a huge effort to clear the fence and I rode both horses forward this time.

'Fortunately I didn't have any problems with the steering or control at the Mitsubishi M at six, which was probably the first real test. For 1997 I felt the best approach was to tackle the three elements on the right-hand side and in fact there was only one rider, Carolyn Ryan Bell and Hooray Henry, who took the left-hand route. The last distance before the final element did walk quite short but I didn't feel this was anything to get too concerned about and in fact both horses jumped it very well and with plenty of power.

'The first time the horses saw a ditch on the course was at the Cirencester Rails which was quite a wide, solidly built parallel with the ditch underneath. I made a mental note on walking the course not to let the horses drift too much to the right, which would make the spread unnecessarily wide. Jumping two big hedges at an acute angle at fence eight, the First Luckington Lane Crossing, can lead to horses running down the side of the second element. I found it best when jumping the course on the anti-clockwise route to put my whip in the left hand over this fence. I had decided to ride strongly towards the fence to make sure both Jack and Arakai jumped well out into the road and attacked the second hedge positively.'

Four strides across Centre Walk they then met the Vicarage Vee on a perfect stride and had one of the best jumps all day through the Galant Hollow at 16. Foot perfect and in attacking style they galloped on through Badminton's notorious Lake and then, as planned, took the left-hand route at the Beaufort Staircase.

'The Centre Walk Hedges are both quite big but not overly complicated. Horses I have ridden over the years have taken a number of different strides between the two hedges depending on what type of horse they were and how onward bound their approach has been. In 1997 both Jack and Harry let me sit quietly and kept their pace at a good, flowing rhythm as they really opened up over them.

'Jumping on a left-hand bend at the Second Luckington Lane Crossing you need to approach the Irish Bank positively but not with too much speed and as the horse pops on and off it is vital that they remain focused on the narrow stile coming out. Jack jumped this fence very well, I pressed on after jumping off the bank, he took two neat strides, remained straight over the stile and we were away with no time lost. The quicker route on the right-hand side left only room for one stride after the bank and I thought it unnecessary to take this risk. If the horse trips off the bank instead of jumping, which can happen, by taking the left side, you have more time to make any adjustments.

'The Carisma Beam at 12 was of maximum dimensions, but I felt it would jump well and not cause too many problems. It was the start of a sequence of fences that had to be jumped as a whole, setting yourself up for each fence in turn. I decided to ride straight to the beam, land straight and then look up to the right for the next fence. Jack in particular jumped fences 12, 13 and 14 very well, losing very little time. To avoid running into problems at the Zig Zag I knew the line was very important from the Carisma Beam. The turn into the fence required balance but the structure of the fence helped to hold you in and once you were fixed on a line it was then a case of riding forward while maintaining that line. I decided to tackle the fence in the middle. A number of riders jumped to the left of it but I felt there was always the possibility of a horse slipping back into the ditch with this route.

'Everything had gone well up to this point on the course and the Vicarage Vee didn't hold too many problems, but as with any corner there is always the chance of the horse running out. Both Jack and Harry took on fences 12, 13 and 14 in great style, and this is when I really started to feel confident.

'It was a short gallop to the Brampton Willow which I considered was one of the few "let up" fences on the course in 1997. However, as with any fence, it is never a good idea to become complacent. The left-hand turn to the fence gave riders the opportunity to set their horses up before the fence and then ride forward being aware that the landing is slightly higher than the take-off. The brush and willow built into the fence also helps the horses to get some height over the jump.

'The approach and speed was very important at the Galant Hollow as I didn't want to end up in a heap on the floor. I actually had a foot-perfect ride through on Jack, probably my best ever. The approach was strong on the turn but with the horse on its hocks and well under control. There was a small stride after the first element before you tackled the ditch, another small stride and then the upright out. This fence has seen a lot of activity over the years but in 1997 most riders appeared to have the measure of it with many more comfortable jumps through than previously. I also thought there was more room through the combination than before.

'A good gallop to the Shooting Butt allowed riders to make up a bit of time and this big, solid fence is one you can really attack. It is always tempting when you have let a horse gallop on to bring them back too much and it is far better to set them up and then keep coming to the fence. I have also known horses put down at this fence with the rider then thrown up around the horse's ears so I didn't want to be leaning too far forward.

'Despite many riders saying the Lake in 1997 was much easier than previously, for me the Badminton Lake will always be a serious challenge and should be treated with respect. The first two elements involved a bounce into the water over well-built, round-topped fences, then three forward strides up on to a jetty and straight off back into the water. I had two excellent rides through on both my horses and was especially pleased with Harry who was a real star. Coming to the Lake you need power and it is no good going the direct route half-heartedly, you must really mean it with plenty of leg on and not stop riding until you reach dry land. I think the rounded tops were kinder but a spread into water is never easy.

'Following very quickly after the Lake were the Mitsubishi Pick Ups. With all the clapping after his effort through the Lake Jack started to trot towards this fence and I had to give him a sharp reminder that he hadn't finished.

'The Beaufort Staircase at 21 was the first fence on the course where I felt I would go different routes with Jack and Harry because of the huge difference in their experience. With Jack I knew he would be able to tackle the three steps up, take one stride and then jump the little house at the top. I felt this could prove just too much for Harry and so decided to turn to the right once I had reached the top of the steps allowing him three strides before jumping the house on the right. I was also well aware that if either horse ran out of steam at the top a quick turn to the right could prevent us incurring any penalties. Over the years I have found that with the younger horses leaving the Lake can often be like starting again and there is a definite need to keep attacking.

Before the cross-country Ian had walked the course several times and had even ventured into the Lake (Tim Smith)

'The Little Badminton Drop was a fence that required more respect than it is often given and choosing your take-off and landing point correctly makes a big difference to success or failure. I always look for the kindest bit of ground to land on because it is very uneven and once you have jumped the fence I allow the horse to free wheel round on its way.'

Ian checked the time on the approach to the Quarry and realising he was

A triumphant Ian completes the cross-country on Arakai (Tim Smith)

Being interviewed after the cross-country (Tim Smith)

up on the clock at this stage stuck to his plan and went the long route. Nineteen ninety-seven saw a completely new look for this fence and I thought that if the time on the clock was looking good, I would take the longer route to avoid the horses having to jump the direct route over the first log. There was a steep drop on the landing side and always the possibility that a young horse might jump too boldly and land at the bottom of the slope. This in fact did happen to Lucy Thompson and Welton Molecule, with Lucy thrown out of the saddle. I felt Jack would have jumped the first log sensibly but on the approach I checked my watch and knew the time was all right so went the long route as I had done with Harry. '

Unbeknown to Ian, Leslie Law and New Flavour, who were just out in front on the course, had run out of steam at the Huntsman's Halo and part of the fence had to be taken down for them to get out. Luckily by the time Ian arrived the fence had been rebuilt and they jumped through without any difficulty.

'The new route through Huntsman's Close required bold riding in over the parallel, then two long strides to a narrow style fence out. As long as the horses jumped boldly in I couldn't see too many problems although the second element did require riders to sit up and take hold to keep horses on a straight line. From the horses' point of view this fence was quite a big effort as they were near the end of the course and were quite tired. The route on leaving Huntsman's Halo affected your route through the Huntsman's Hangovers, which could be jumped on three long strides.

'There was then a short gallop to the Colt Feeder with the finish in sight and, although inviting, this fence was nevertheless quite substantial. Home at last and on both rides I felt a great sense of achievement and relief. The take-off in front of the final fence had been improved which was a help for the horses and gave a better jump. Going through the finish at Badminton is always a real high and this year was especially so with Harry's round giving me so much satisfaction.'

Maintaining the lead at this stage with David O'Connor in second and Mary King in third, Ian was rushed off to a press conference to be greeted by a host of congratulations. Said Ian: 'I had two extremely good rides. The main difference was the ground conditions at the start and the end of the day and Jack ran away with me on the steeplechase slightly.'

When asked about Stanwick Ghost's show-jumping reputation, Ian said: 'I

Sunday morning before the start of the vets' inspection (Tim Smith)

was in this position last year. We have worked very hard on the show-jumping with Lars Sederholm and Jack does try but at the same time doesn't really care. We have been trying to get him to use his back, but will have to wait and see what tomorrow brings. He has been jumping better all year and if any horse deserves to win he does. I would rather be in this position and have a couple of show-jumps down than not be here at all, but I have to admit whereas on the cross-country he tucks his legs up carefully out of the way this doesn't happen in the show-jumping.' A lot of interest was shown in Arakai's performance and Ian said he had all the ability to make a top-class horse. 'The aim at this stage in his career is to get him experienced in the atmosphere, especially in the dressage. I think he is possibly the classiest horse I have ever ridden across country, for sheer ability, and is very brave and intelligent.'

The night of 10 May proved somewhat sleepless for the team. An unsettled Sunday morning greeted riders and spectators who turned out in force to watch the final trot-up and with both horses looking in wonderful condition they passed the inspection without any worries.

As the parade of competitors was about to start at 2.30 p.m. the heavens opened in spectacular style and by the time it had finished everyone was

Ian and Stanwick Ghost at the trot-up (Tim Smith)

Vicky and Stephanie waiting for the end of Jack's show-jumping round (Tim Smith)

soaked to the skin. Ian entered the ring on Harry to a warm welcome and was pleased that he had a good round with just 5.25 penalties – the result of a rail falling at the second and a quarter of a time fault being accrued. Lady Vestey was thrilled with Arakai's overall performance at his first Badminton. It was then an agonizing wait with Sharon keeping Jack on the move before the final round of the day. Blyth Tait and William Fox-Pitt had both risen up the order with good clear rounds and Mary King escaped with just one fence down before David O'Connor and Custom Made jumped the round of their life to go clear.

Ian got on Jack with about five riders to go and quietly warmed him up as the practice arena became more and more deserted. Prospects were not looking too good, as he appeared unsure of leaving the ground and giving the fence any real height. But Jenny quietly altered the fence and the sun came out just before they entered the arena.

David O'Connor slapped palms with Ian as he entered the arena but sadly it didn't bring him the luck he needed. The tension mounted for the third day running and close connections found it impossible to watch the round but knew it was all over as the noise from the stands grew, Jack hitting five fences and dropping to 13th place just ahead of Harry.

It left everyone feeling very down including the British public who had been behind Ian all the way. Said Jenny: 'We would have understood if a couple of fences had fallen but five was very disappointing.' A jubilant David O'Connor was generous in his praise for Ian and said his heart went out to Ian whom he had watched so closely over the years and admired greatly.

Following the disappointment at Badminton, there was further bad news on the way when a routine check on Stanwick Ghost at Newmarket revealed a leg injury. Despite trotting-up sound on the Monday morning in front of the selectors for the Open Europeans problems were diagnosed a day later. The check-up at Newmarket on the Tuesday showed he would need time off and both Ian and his connections realised Stanwick Ghost would be out of action for a year and would miss the Open Europeans at Burghley in September.

The 1997 Open European Championships

'Ian is a true team member. Without Arakai or Stanwick Ghost, who is out of action, Britain's challenge looks a little less threatening.'

SUE BENSON WRITING IN *EVENTING MAGAZINE* ON THE
LONG LIST FOR THE OPEN EUROPEAN CHAMPIONSHIPS
AT BURGHLEY IN 1997

During the early part of the summer season it was looking doubtful whether Ian would have a ride at Burghley. Lord and Lady Vestey had voiced concern over whether the inexperienced Arakai was ready for the challenge and Stanwick Ghost's leg problems, which came to light after Badminton, had put him out of the reckoning. Much was written in the press in the few weeks before the championships and after Arakai's good round at the final trial at Thirlestane in August Lord and Lady Vestey gave the go-ahead for him to be considered.

Ian's experience and many years at the top of the sport was considered a great asset to any team, helping to pull everyone together and creating the strong, focused vision required for a major championships. Running on home ground, Britain was able to field a 12-strong squad with a top six chosen for a coveted team place. Along with Ian and Harry in the top six came Mary King and Star Appeal, a winner at Burghley the previous year, William Fox-Pitt and the consistent Cosmopolitan II, Anne-Marie Evans and Dutch Treat, Kristina Gifford and General Jock, and Chris Bartle with Word Perfect II, a winner of the final trial.

The few weeks before the Europeans were fraught with anxiety. After

Ian and Arakai at the trot-up (Tim Smith)

Arakai's solid performance at Thirlestane which showed how much he had matured, the dressage mark being well up with the leaders, Ian suffered a bad fall at Blair with Mr Mackinnon, before his luck changed at Blenheim where he finished fifth on Lady Hartington's good young horse The Moose.

As the 1997 Burghley Open European Championships approached Mark Phillips wrote in *Horse and Hound*: 'It had been rumoured before Thirlestane that Lord and Lady Vestey's Arakai might be available for selection if he went well. He didn't just go well, he was outstanding as he skipped over the fences in the capable hands of Ian Stark, with an ease, that only the great horses enjoy.'

Ian had won four European team golds as well as the individual championship in 1991 so there was a lot to play for going into the 1997 event. Alan Smith of the *Daily Telegraph* wrote: 'Ian's record in championships glitters like few other riders including four team golds and the individual in the 1991 Europeans. Such well-practised expertise will surely outweigh the lack of mileage of the young but improving Arakai.'

Britain entered the fold as defending European and World Champions and started as one of the favourites. Burghley 1997 saw one of the strongest fields

Warming up before the dressage (Tim Smith)

ever competing and the British team went to the Europeans determined to put the record straight after the disappointment of the Olympics.

Following the trot-up on the Wednesday the team was announced as Mary King with the 1996 Burghley champion Star Appeal, Ian on Arakai, Chris Bartle making his eventing team debut on Word Perfect II and William Fox-Pitt on Cosmopolitan II. Running in that order Mary was to go first, riding the bold and courageous Star Appeal in the hope their performance would get the team off to a good start.

Working Arakai early on the Thursday morning before his dressage test Ian's main hope was that he would remain calm and obedient throughout and not show the tense side of his character which Ian had worked so hard to remove. At 9.32 a.m. on the Thursday, Mary and Star Appeal performed their usual polished test to score 47.2 penalties and get the team off to the start they hoped for. Three hours later and with Ian on board, Arakai was brought up to the arena with Barbara Slane Fleming, Ian's dressage trainer, on hand for any last minute advice. After some slow gentle work and with Arakai's lucky thistle quarter marks in place, Ian entered the arena on a calm-looking horse.

With hardly any breeze and the stands silent Ian started his test. Each movement flowed and everyone held their breath as Ian went to work and the horse co-operated. But for a slight mistake at the second flying change, Arakai performed the test of his life to score 47.8 penalties to huge applause. Mary's usual stylish performance and Ian's dream effort had left them in third and fourth positions at this stage. Swamped by members of the press as he left the arena, Ian was overwhelmed with the test and delighted with the score, which was much improved from the 66 they scored at Badminton in the spring.

Said Ian: 'My boots kept slipping in the stirrups but Arakai was wonderful. He started to show off a bit and began to trust me and understand it was possible which was a real breakthrough. As he grew in confidence he became more secure. Forty-five minutes before the test all I wanted to do was sleep in the lorry but then when I heard the mark I couldn't believe it.'

Britain's morale remained on a high throughout Friday when Chris Bartle and William Fox-Pitt put in the tests expected to keep Britain out in front at the end of the first phase. Chris and Word Perfect II scored a magnificent 43.40 while William and Cosmopolitan II, not renowned for being easy in the dressage, finished on 45.20. Their performances left Great Britain on 135.80 followed closely by the United States on 141.20 with New Zealand just 0.40

Vicky applies the lucky thistle to Arakai's quarters (Tim Smith)

penalties adrift so there was everything to play for at this stage. On the individual front Ian and Arakai held 12th position going into the cross-country which was more than he had ever dared hope for.

Being an Open European Championships brought a number of complications with a series of medals and awards to be won but the British team had its sights firmly fixed on becoming the European team gold medallists as they went into the speed and endurance phase. A day of blustery wind, a little sunshine and a few showers, greeted Ian and the other team members on cross-country day. Walking Mike Tucker's superbly designed course, Ian's main concern came at fence four, the Leaf Pit Kennel Tree Stumps, an odd-looking fence standing three feet eleven inches high and difficult to get to on the approach. This was a big test for both horse and rider so early on in the course and Ian was well aware of the danger of incurring penalties at this stage.

The new Lion Bridge complex had also created much discussion coming so soon after the Kissing Seats. The direct route in would mean horses launching themselves downhill into the water over an imposing hanging log. Taking the left route which provided a simple, if not small drop into the water would see riders hauling their mounts over to the left with split-second reactions needed to set up the correct approach. Once in the water riders took a left-hand turn to negotiate either a boat under the bridge or two fences further to the right which riders quickly realised was unnecessary.

Mary got the team off to a flying start coming home both clear and inside the time while also bringing back plenty of useful information for the team. Asked what his first impression of the course had been, Ian replied: 'Mike Tucker's course is full of new ideas and is very imaginative, though more serious than expected.' Those last four words were echoed by many riders who felt the task was much more a four-star level than a three-star track.

The influence of the cross-country certainly meant the competition was much more than just a dressage event and riders had great respect for the track which required a bold approach and quick-thinking actions through the various combinations put in their way. Ian felt the course was beautifully presented with questions coming one after another which gave riders few opportunities to let their concentration lapse.

Ian set out on phase A at 11.06 a.m. to a great cheer as Arakai, looking fit and well, kept a close watch on the crowds that lined the track. Starting phase

D – the cross-country – just under one hour and 20 minutes later everything had gone to plan so far. Ruth Day, Lord and Lady Vestey's head girl, was on hand to help Vicky while Lady Vestey had travelled to Burghley to cheer on Ian.

Following Mary, Bruce Davidson for the United States arrived home inside the time, while Andrew Nicholson for New Zealand who had finished ninth after the dressage had a run out at the influential Dairy Cobwebs fence. Ian and Arakai set off in their usual attacking style, safely negotiating the first two fences before taking the direct route at the Leaf Pit Log. They then opted for a slightly longer approach to fence four, the Leaf Pit Kennel Tree Stumps to make sure they had that one safely out of the way.

Ian had said that the Leaf Pit Log with a steep drop required the rider to collect the horse in front of the fence while also riding boldly and positively before gathering the reins again for the next fence. Any problems encountered there in Arakai's mind were safely restored at the Newage Ditch before swinging left-handed to the Land Rover Lane Crossing at six. A big, firm, upright hedge going in was followed by a slope down to a ditch, before bouncing out over another hedge. Ian had been instructed not to take the corner route here, the risk being too great for the team. Ian recalls: 'Arakai jumped the final hedge at the Land Rover Lane Crossing rather awkwardly but I knew he was going and rode strongly out over the final element with his natural athletic ability saving us from any problems. I carried on over Thomson's Wall and the Log Trakhener at eight before I was suddenly held on the course as Kibah Medallion and Astrid van Leeuwen for the Netherlands had fallen at the Trout Hatchery. By mistake I reset my watch to zero instead of stopping it and after that I just rode as fast as possible and thank heavens finished within the time with a brilliant round from the horse. He was incredibly bold and athletic but it didn't help not knowing the correct time. I was held for about five minutes and then had to face the big Timberyard Cordwood which Arakai tackled for fun.'

On they galloped over the Waterloo Dragon, a new fence for 1997, before taking the Water Cascade in their stride and then running downhill towards the Trout Hatchery. An upright wall in, Ian rode strongly on the approach giving Arakai the necessary confidence to jump in before veering to the right-hand side to jump out. Once across the 30-yard stretch of water that gradually became deeper, Ian rode Arakai strongly up the step to bounce over

Safely over fence 26, the Jubilee Brush (Tim Smith)

the wall under the canopy. Hitting this element hard, Ian stuck like glue to the saddle before leaping out over the final fence and into the second water showing the crowd that he was full of running and relishing the task.

At Capability's Cutting, Arakai was very neat taking the direct route before galloping on to the Dairy Cobwebs where he remained straight as a die and kept the constant rhythm Ian was trying to maintain. Setting Arakai up for the Kissing Seat after he had run on boldly downhill, Ian got this safely out of the way before taking two strides and then launching himself over the log. A spectacular jump and they were over the boat fence to great cheers and were by now well over two-thirds round.

Says Ian: 'Arakai was so neat, he just didn't want to touch anything. Coming into the Lion Bridge I could see all the skid marks from the other horses and began to try to slow down. I was coming on two strides and we were a long way off, I shouted at the horse and he went up so high we flew over the log and it was one hell of a drop, he was fabulous and tried his heart out. The whole course rode very big. I had every confidence in Arakai, a lot of people felt he was rather inexperienced but I wouldn't have been there if I had thought he wouldn't be able to cope. He had gone very well at Badminton and was proving very bold with a fantastic jump.'

Nearing the end of the course, Ian and Arakai took the long route through the Burghley Garden fence in the arena, opting out of the bounce route which was riding quite short. After a superb effort Ian finished inside the optimum time on 11 minutes 17 seconds with just 11 seconds to spare. His good round also left him just 0.6 penalties adrift of Mary and Star Appeal.

Ian's cross-country prowess had come into its own with a masterly piece of riding round the course. The hold-up was Arakai's first experience of such an occurrence and everyone was pleased with how well he coped with the situation. The horse had remained full of concentration throughout, showing his true scope and ability while Ian had reacted instinctively over some of the more complex combinations, coming up with the answers when it was required. A nervous horse at the best of times, it helped to have both Vicky and Ruth on hand to look after Arakai who is much better with people he knows. The difference in his mental attitude at Burghley to that in the spring at Badminton was incredible as he showed a more mature outlook on what was happening around him. Not having Jack nearby was also a bonus as he was much more relaxed and focused, not always looking for his stable mate.

Sadly Chris Bartle and Word Perfect's round came to an abrupt halt with a fall at fence six before William brought the team back into the lead with a confident clear on Cosmopolitan to a great cheer. Down on the clock as he entered the arena, William took the quick route at the Burghley Garden fence to come home clear and inside the time. With the top three scores to count this left Britain on 140.2 penalties at the end of the speed and endurance phase with William, Mary and Ian lying in third, fourth and fifth places. New Zealand and Australia followed while the United States dropped to fifth.

The following morning after the exhilaration of the cross-country the team had a major scare when Cosmopolitan was held by the ground jury and it took a third trot-up and much encouragement from the crowd before the horse was eventually passed to great applause.

'After Badminton I thought that Arakai was the best I had ever ridden and his round at Burghley confirmed it,' says Ian. 'I was lying fifth after the cross-country which was great but you can never be too sure how much this has taken out of the horse. The course was quite a big test for Arakai and I wondered how much energy he would have for the show-jumping. He is usually a very good show-jumper but after the cross-country I felt it didn't matter if I had the odd pole down although I didn't want to let the team down.'

As the show-jumping approached the atmosphere became increasingly tense and when Chris and Word Perfect jumped a good clear it was just what everyone needed. Kenneth Clawson was on hand to help Ian with Arakai at the practice fence and they gave everyone a fright when he fell through a parallel, staying on his feet in the process, but Ian could have done without the mistake. A more generous time allowance in the show-jumping brought some much improved rounds and silence fell over the arena as they entered. Despite their efforts Ian was out of luck as the horse's inexperience showed and two fences fell, Arakai being slightly unnerved by the crowds. Mary and Star Appeal followed Ian and when two fences hit the deck the British lead was gradually slipping away. Having dominated in the dressage and cross-country Britain appeared vulnerable in the show-jumping with just William to go. As he entered the arena the sun shone and Cosmopolitan took the course in his stride as a cool-looking William came home clear.

Ian was delighted with Arakai's tenth place. Mary was eighth and William overall third and European silver medal winner. Ian recalls: 'Arakai is still

Lap of honour: (left to right) *William Fox-Pitt on Cosmopolitan* II, *Mary King on Star Appeal, Ian on Arakai and Chris Bartle on Word Perfect* II (Tim Smith)

relatively young and I didn't feel there was any real problem to overcome. The horse did everything I asked of him. He was exceptional for his age and lack of experience. At fences two and three which he hit he felt a bit flat behind, there was so much for him to concentrate on, towards the end of the course he was much more settled and jumped well. William did a marvellous job and thoroughly deserved the medals he claimed. It is always very rewarding being on a team and to win the gold medal was wonderful.'

Team silver winners: (left to right) *Ginny Holgate on Priceless, Ian on Oxford Blue, Tiny Clapham on Windjammer and Lucinda Green on Regal Realm* (Claire Davies)

$$5$$

Olympic Endeavours and Competing Abroad

'*Los Angeles was just a whirl of excitement, Ian's career had really taken off and the whole event was quite a blur.*'

JENNY STARK

Ian has the remarkable record of competing at the last four Olympics. The selectors first considered him for Los Angeles in 1984 with Oxford Blue and Sir Wattie. It was Oxford Blue who was eventually chosen, with Wattie waiting in the wings. Four years later and by now well known and much respected, Ian was there again, this time on Wattie at the Seoul Olympics when they returned with both team and individual silver medals.

Barcelona followed in 1992 with Murphy Himself getting the chance to show his ability. Spun at the inspection on the final day due to a strained fetlock, Britain's hopes of a team medal went by the board much to everyone's disappointment. Ian had taken both Murphy and Glenburnie to Barcelona but chose Murphy after seeing the cross-country course. Atlanta 1996 provided an Olympic trip for Stanwick Ghost and his owners Lord and Lady Hartington. But after a first-rate dressage Ian and Stanwick Ghost's efforts fell apart with a fall at the water complex on the cross-country course.

Los Angeles 1984

Looking back at his first Olympics at Los Angeles Ian says: 'Everything happened so quickly. The selectors decided I should ride Oxford Blue and the whole event was an incredible experience as I was very much the new boy on the team. People behaved as if I had just started riding. I hadn't been competing in the south a great deal and at that stage I was made to ride to order and had time faults on the cross-country but no one knew what to expect really. Just before the trip Oxford Blue managed to get a rub on his saddle patch which meant I had to ride him bareback for several weeks. Jumping and galloping him without a saddle wasn't funny as he had a very high wither!

'When I was announced as a member of the team I never really took it in that I was one of the five selected. At the final trial at Castle Ashby there were ten riders and 16 horses in contention. We did our dressage on the Saturday and the horses were examined by the selection committee and the team vet. There was a ball on the Saturday night for the Olympic Appeal Fund and then on the Sunday morning we show-jumped.

'Oxford Blue jumped clear but Sir Wattie had a fence down which was my fault as I asked him for a long stride. The cross-country was later in the day and Wattie had the fastest time to finish sixth, while Oxford Blue was the only horse inside the time to take second. The horses were vetted again at 7 a.m. the following morning and we were then told there would be a five-minute break so we went off for a coffee. The atmosphere was quite tense and the selection committee never has an easy task.

'It was quite unusual to have so many good, fit horses, and it had taken them a long time to get to the stage of choosing the five riders. It was fantastic news and at that point I just hoped the horses would stay sound. I was on the team with Tiny Clapham, Lucinda Green, Ginny Elliot (then Holgate), with Robert Lemieux as reserve. I had my first experience of team training with the Hugh Russells at Wylye in Wiltshire. Everyone was helped by Ferdi Eilberg and Pat Burgess and it was wonderful to have such support on hand.

'Lady Hugh gave me a lot of help on the cross-country once I had got over her intimidating manner but the whole team training session was actually quite a blur as our days were planned and we went from one activity to another. Just before the horses actually left for the airport, a ministry vet wasn't going to allow Oxford Blue to travel as he was covered in old ringworm scars and warts. It was an extremely anxious moment. When we arrived at Santa Anita, a racecourse that was being used for the dressage and show-jumping, it was nice to find the house Heather Holgate, Ginny's mum, had organised for us was just a short distance away from the stables.

'The cross-country however required a lengthy trip south to the Fairbanks ranch but the climate was much better with a cooling breeze which helped both the horses and riders. Jenny and Dame Jean Maxwell-Scott came out to lend their support and Claire Davies was grooming for me. The whole experience and run-up to Los Angeles happened very quickly and there wasn't a lot of time to take everything in. Once we arrived, it was simply a case of getting on with the job and doing our best. Robbie and Wattie had both travelled well which was a relief as neither had flown before and it was somewhat worrying especially as the plane was very hot, loaded full with horses and equipment. Having a base not far from the racecourse with a swimming pool to keep our temperatures down was a help and the *chef d'equipe* Malcolm Wallace really held the whole operation together. The tight security at Los Angeles came as quite a shock.'

Never an easy job, the team was chosen as Ginny Holgate on Priceless, Tiny Clapham on Windjammer, Ian on Robbie and Lucinda Green with Regal Realm. Out of all the horses Robert Lemieux's The Gamesmaster had travelled the worst and everyone felt for Robert when he was left off the team. However his spirits remained high and he was a great help to everyone.

'During the dressage the heat was unbearable but when I finished on the same score as Ginny with Priceless it was wonderful. Jenny travelled out with Dame Jean and came to Fairbanks to watch the cross-country with busloads of people. Ginny got the team off to a great start with a polished performance before Tiny had a fall at the water complex. As this was my first Olympics I was desperate to do well and set off on Oxford Blue hoping the same fate wouldn't befall us.

'He hit the second fence hard but luckily we stayed upright and the rest of the round went without incident. Lucinda and Regal Realm held the team together with a real attacking round before we returned to Santa Anita racecourse for the final phase. The Americans were leading with the British team holding second place at this stage and I suddenly became very aware of how crucial it was we all went well in the show-jumping.

'Ted Edgar was on hand to help at the practice fence. Lucinda, Ginny and Tiny all jumped clear but I found Robbie extremely tired after his cross-country round and had a difficult time with him as he touched nearly every fence. Nevertheless team silver was ours and the award ceremony is something I will never forget.

'Much of the time during the Olympics I had very little contact with Jenny or Dame Jean as the security was so tight, and once the competition was over

Los Angeles celebrations: (left to right) *chef d'equipe Malcolm Wallace, Ian, Ginny Holgate, Lucinda Green, Tiny Clapham*

they returned home and arranged a party in Ashkirk Hall. Somehow they managed to keep it a surprise, but I'm sure I wasn't the easiest person to deal with. I was hurried on to a flight after a press conference in London wondering what all the fuss was about not realising there would be all these people waiting for us when we finally arrived home.

'I had been given numerous bottles of alcohol at the press conference and was laden down as we got into the car with my mother, Stephanie and Tim. When Jenny drove into the reception I was shocked to say the least as the crowds were cheering and I found it hard to believe so many people had turned out. The house and stables had also been decorated and I couldn't believe so many people had gone to all the effort.'

Seoul 1988

'The build up to Seoul was very different from Los Angeles with all the pressure resting on Wattie. Korea was a totally non-horsey nation and the facilities they had developed were quite fantastic. The stables were second to none,' recalls Ian.

'I was fortunate to have Jenny, Dame Jean and David and Alix Stevenson from The Edinburgh Woollen Mill to shout and encourage everyone on. Alison Duthie was grooming Wattie and the team included Ginny Leng with Master Craftsman, Mark Phillips on Cartier and Karen Dixon with Get Smart, while Lorna Clarke and Fearliath Mor were reserves.

'Jenny and the others were on an organised tour which in itself led to one adventure after another. One of the party was an old war veteran who insisted on kidnapping the bus and taking everyone to the war zone. Suddenly they ended up in no man's land surrounded by soldiers which was quite an experience for all concerned. The party stayed in what everyone believed were brothels as the government had block booked all the major hotels expecting a huge demand which never arose as they were so expensive. The trip to Seoul provided everyone with many laughable incidents including the occasion when an official who was organising owners' passes decided that Jenny, Dame Jean and David and Alix Stevenson all looked the same and asked if all four could squeeze together on the same identity photograph.

'In 1984 my inclusion on the team had been a surprise to many people, as well as myself but four years later I was determined to try and take in the whole Olympics scene so that I could actually go home having remembered clearly what had happened. We had a lot of problems at the Korean customs with team members missed off the computer while I was down as female which gave everyone a laugh.

'I remember looking at the many places you could eat in the Olympic Village and deciding nothing looked particularly appetising but this gave us a good excuse to eat out when we got the opportunity. The horses were very well catered for with superb facilities at Kwachon, big airy stables and sandy hacking around the equestrian park. We were fortunate that the horses travelled very well and after the two days of quarantine we were able to start work with them. Travelling from where we were staying to the stadium was quite a nightmare and when our mini-bus driver caused a collision we wondered if we would get there in one piece. There were a number of times we got lost but he always tried to be helpful and we always saw the funny side.

'I had finished in fifth place in the dressage and knew I needed a good cross-country round to improve my position. Mark on Cartier was unlucky when the rain came bucketing down during his effort but Karen and Ginny both performed very good tests.

'We had a one-and-a-quarter hour trip to Wondang for the cross-country and although the fences were not the biggest I had seen their siting made them quite difficult and the undulating terrain was very tiring and jarring on the horses. There were various alterations made to the course after our first walk, with the removal of a five-yard bounce with a drop at fences 27 and 28. Taking the first element out was welcomed by everyone as it came at the end of the course and wasn't necessary.

'We all felt luck had deserted us when Cartier had to be withdrawn in the ten-minute box with pulled muscles in his quarters and this left Karen first to go for the team. She did an excellent job and was unfortunate to part company with Get Smart at the second water. I was thrilled with Wattie who gave me a brilliant ride especially at a difficult corner fence and an "into space" fence. It was very hot and humid on the cross-country and the horses had to be hosed down in a cooling shed after competing. I thought I was going to pass out when I had finished because I was so exhausted and Wattie was very tired.'

After the cross-country Ian and Wattie were in third position following an excellent round in which Ian put to good use the horse's ability to cut corners in a bid to save time and following the show-jumping Ian clinched the silver medal.

Says Jenny: 'When Ian came out of the ring he could hardly speak and was almost in tears. I was able to help Ian in the practice ring and he was very nervous before competing, especially from the team angle, as it was so close. It was a real panic beforehand in case he knocked any fences down and when they went clear we had to wait to see if he would get bronze or silver.'

The team came away with the silver medal. 'The support group which goes to all the main events had tried to arrange a room in Seoul for supporters to meet and entertain,' says Jenny. 'However, when they got out there, the Korean authorities were very difficult and eventually we just took over a corner of the grandstand and had our party there. We decorated it with British flags and it was a great success.'

'I remember phoning home after winning the medals and speaking to Stephanie,' says Ian. 'All she could tell me about were two new kittens Sooty and Sweep that had been acquired. She jumped at the chance to tell me while I was in such a good mood, knowing I don't really like cats.

'Wattie arrived home with his groom Alison Duthie and we were quite relieved it was all over. It had been a long build-up to the competition with arrangements being made since the beginning of the year and it was good to retire Wattie sound and to end his career on such a high note.'

Ian returned home to a hero's welcome when almost 300 well-wishers, friends and family turned out to greet him. This time Ian knew about the party at Ashkirk Hall but was staggered by the crowd who had gathered. Ian remembers: 'I was quite overwhelmed. It didn't feel like four years since I had a similar welcome. Oxford Blue had taken me to my first Olympics and Wattie had put me where I was that day. Because we had decided to retire him it was the end of an era and quite sad but there was a lot of celebrating.

'When I returned from the Olympics my head was still full of the closing ceremony in Seoul which was so exciting and watching videos brings back a lot of happy memories. Sharing that special atmosphere with thousands of people from all over the world is quite incredible.'

Barcelona 1992

Barcelona in 1992 was the first Olympics when Jenny actually got to see quite a lot of Ian as she stayed in the house the British team had rented for the cross-country. The alternative two-hour bus journey didn't bear thinking about and using the house as a base made life much easier. David and Alix Stevenson weren't so lucky and patiently endured the lengthy travelling everyday.

Says Jenny: 'Ian had been doing very well on a big coloured horse called Mix N' Match in between Seoul and Barcelona. He was by the thoroughbred Tudor Diver and it had always been Ian's intention to take the horse to the Olympics but after an offer came forward for the horse we found it too difficult to turn down and he was sold. By now Ian had formed a good partnership with Murphy and Glenburnie who were both in contention.

'Just before the final trial at Savernake Forest Ian had a slight panic that he might not have given the horses enough outings but in the end both horses went well and Murphy stole the limelight with a win in his section. We had

Mix N' Match was a horse Ian had thought might be an Olympic contender

moved down to be based at Stowell Park. It was better placed geographically for all the Barcelona preparations and there were the fundraising events to attend and team training to go through. There was also concern about the outbreak of equine diseases such as African Horse Sickness and an equine flu in the area we were travelling to, but the initial worry was overcome with constant reassurances and checks over any developments. Some trips just seem to be awkward from the start and everything about our visit to Barcelona had some kind of problem.

'I travelled over to support Ian with David and Alix Stevenson but the circumstances were always against us. This started with a traffic jam, delayed flight and managing to miss the first trot-up. After a long day and what seemed like an equally long bus journey back to the hotel in the evening there was no dinner left because we were too late. Luckily I managed to escape and was able to stay with the riders. The competition itself ran very efficiently and as expected there was a lot of security to contend with especially as there were bomb scares just a few days before the three-day event.'

Ian had captured the European Championships at Punchestown the previous year on Glenburnie and in the early stages of Olympic preparation was unsure which horse would be chosen. A last minute withdrawal by Ginny Leng and Master Craftsman due to injury left the squad of Mary King with King William, Richard Walker on Jacana, Karen Dixon with Get Smart and Ian with his two greys.

'The event was soon underway and panic quickly set in when Richard Walker's dressage coat was left behind while he was working in. A last minute dash to get it to him on time was made but he nearly had to go in wearing Andrew Nicholson's tailcoat carrying the New Zealand flag. All the riders completed good tests, sending them off to a strong start before the cross-country. They all coped very well with the baking heat and Murphy produced one of his bests tests ever, for his last performance,' recalls Ian.

Up until seeing the cross-country course at El Mantanya golf club Ian refused to make a decision on which horse to run. But on viewing the huge course with a tiring number of complex combinations he felt Murphy would be able to cope best as long as he could manoeuvre him along the tight twisty tracks. After the dressage Murphy and Ian lay in second place individually while the team were in the lead. As anchorman, Ian had a big task on his shoulders going into the cross-country. Clears, albeit slow ones, by Mary and

The Barcelona squad: (left to right) *Richard Walker, Ian, Karen Dixon, Mary King*
(Barbara Thomson)

Murphy (left) *in his stable at Barcelona*

Karen had held the effort together after Richard Walker and Jacana had parted company at the second water complex. Ian's round on Murphy will be remembered for years to come. The horse, in his usual bold, attacking style, ate up the course but in doing so he hit fence 18 – a bank and rails out of the water – hard.

Coming home with 36.4 time penalties, Ian had struggled to control the hard-pulling grey and hadn't enjoyed the ride at all. As if he knew Murphy's career had come to the final stage, Ian had made the difficult decision to retire him after Barcelona and when he was spun at the final vet's inspection their wonderful years together came to an abrupt, heartbreaking halt. A horse who always thrilled on the cross-country, Murphy was out of the Olympics and so Britain lost her chance of gaining a medal at Barcelona.

'We had always known that this competition would be his finale. There were moments out on the cross-country when his sheer brilliance sparkled as always. But, there were also those split seconds when you are reminded that a horse cannot go on forever, however brilliant he is,' said Ian.

'Having Murphy spun on the final day wasn't the way Ian or anyone else wanted the horse to be remembered because there had been so many good times together and it was a bitter blow for us to handle,' recalls Jenny. 'His score was desperately needed for the team and it was decided he should be presented but Murphy just did not trot up in his usual extravagant way. Normally he was pulling Ian's arms out, but that time it was not the case. He looked quiet which was just not like Murphy.

'I didn't particularly enjoy Barcelona and felt Ian wasn't on his best form. There are times when everything goes well from start to finish and it is a particularly good event, but for us Barcelona wasn't one of those occasions. Mark Holliday, who was so good with Murphy, was looking after him and we felt very sorry for him. The highs and lows of eventing always backfire on the grooms and the ultimate disappointment of failure is often felt most by the people looking after the horses.

'The end result of the three-day event in Barcelona was great for the crowds but not for Britain and our talk of staying for the closing ceremony of the Games evaporated and we decided to return home and get on with working towards the next event.'

Atlanta 1996

Atlanta 1996 was a special occasion for Ian and Jenny when Lord and Lady Hartington, owners of Ian's Olympic ride Stanwick Ghost, offered to pay for Stephanie and Tim to join them for the event.

Says Jenny: 'Despite it not being the most successful trip as far as results go, the trip to Atlanta was wonderful having Stephanie and Tim there. We stayed in a motel with Ian based just across the road and out of all four Olympics Ian has been involved with it must go down as one of the most relaxed. The theme parks and nightlife were quite amazing and when the Starks decided to go on a ride which dropped you from a great height I was rather pleased I had opted out, it looked quite horrific.

'The team of Ian, William Fox-Pitt with Cosmopolitan II, Gary Parsonage on Magic Rouge and Karen Dixon with Too Smart were on a real high, when Ian and Stanwick Ghost led the dressage after a fabulous test. But his fall in

The support team at Atlanta (Dr Jonathan Hunt)

Ian achieved his best-ever dressage mark of 35.2 penalties at a three-day event on Stanwick Ghost at Atlanta (Bob Langrish)

the water on the cross-country left everyone feeling very deflated.'

Ian's dressage of 35.2 penalties was followed by William on 49 which everyone felt was somewhat harshly marked. Gary finished his test rather relieved, scoring 62.6, while Karen was delighted when the exuberant Too Smart settled sufficiently to produce a commendable 43.6 penalties.

With the United States in the lead the British team was holding its own just 4.8 behind while New Zealand claimed third. Roger Haller had built a superb course for the team event, the individual running over a separate track and great care had been taken to make sure the horses were all carefully checked over with concerns about their welfare in the heat.

Ian's wonderful lead came to an end with his fall at the 11th fence on the cross-country course after Stanwick Ghost fell up the bank and then tipped Ian heavily over the succeeding fence. Once both horse and rider were back on their feet they carried on none the worse for their fall but everyone back at base felt for them.

Following Ian, William and Cosmopolitan came to grief at fence eight, stopping at the second element before Gary and Magic Rouge put in a great jumping effort to go clear, a feat similarly achieved by Karen. By now the team was out of the reckoning, finishing the day in sixth place.

The final phase dawned but only Karen and Too Smart could manage a clear over a testing course, which caused plenty of problems. Caroline Powell, who was looking after Stanwick Ghost, had spent the hours in between the cross-country and show-jumping working to get the horse through the final inspection and although this was a success, the horse, still rather sore, claimed three show- jumping poles during his round.

Atlanta was neither Ian's nor Britain's finest Olympic effort with overall fortunes being rather bleak. And once the competition was over Ian returned home to help Stephanie prepare for her final trial for the Junior European team at Dauntsey. Making it through to the team, Stephanie and Go Bust fell at the water during the Championships at Blair and the press wrote that both the Starks' team efforts in 1996 were claimed by water jumps.

COMPETING ABROAD

Competing abroad has become second nature to Ian but Jenny remembers his first trip to Achselschwang in Germany very clearly. Long awaited, the travelling seemed to go on and on and they spent many hours in the lorry before reaching their destination. Tim and Stephanie had been left at home with Ian's mother and much to everyone's concern Tim had decided Jenny must have died and couldn't understand where she had gone. So bad was his longing to see Jenny again that Ian's mother took him to the doctor in the vain hope he would be able to help. For Jenny the trip was a turning point in her trying to be all things to everyone and she realised it was going to be a difficult task both caring for the children and assisting Ian with his career. From then on the aim was to try and always have people working for them who liked children and who could step into the breach when required so that Stephanie and Tim never felt as if they were being left. The trips abroad continued to be vital steps in Ian's career but continued to be major efforts and mammoth organisational nightmares. Four to six trips are made each year and although this may not sound a great deal slotted in around all the other activities they remain quite demanding with all the travelling involved.

Horses have taken Ian to far-reaching parts of the globe and one of the first 'exotic' trips he made was to Phoenix, Arizona in the United States in February 1985. Recalls Ian: 'I got a telephone call at the beginning of the year asking me if I would like to fly to Phoenix to ride in an event they were holding there. At first I thought it was a joke but when the tickets arrived I had to take the offer a bit more seriously.

'The thought of leaving snowy Scotland at the end of February seemed too good to be true. But leaving all the horses for Jenny and the staff to do did mean they would be very busy with all the fittening work and when I returned it would be straight into the spring events. The trip out lasted 19 hours but to be greeted by the hot, sunny weather made everything seem very worthwhile.

'At first glance I hadn't a clue where they would hold an event, the only place I could see being a vast desert covered in dangerous looking cacti and I didn't immediately relish the thought of galloping past such obstacles on a horse I wouldn't know very well. All my concerns were soon put to rest by the efficient organisation of the Southwest Equestrian Athletic Training Association who were a great bunch of people putting all their efforts into making the event a success. They ran both an Open Intermediate and a three-day event without the roads and tracks and steeplechase a week later. I rode a horse called Robin Hood which I was lent for the two events and really enjoyed the experience. The idea of running the event was to gain more

A fall on the cross-country at Gawler in 1986 for Ian on Oxford Blue put them out of the running (The Advertiser)

publicity for horse trials in the area and it also raised funds for cerebral palsy charities. It was a great boost for the sport and as one of my first invitations overseas it was wonderful to be there. From the sponsorship viewpoint the organisers certainly made sure everything ran smoothly and everyone was well looked after with a golf tournament, parties and a chance for the sponsors to mix with the riders.

'The cross-country course was a true advanced track but I was pleased to find it wasn't too technical which was good as quite a lot of the horses and riders were competing in an Advanced competition for the first time. Robin Hood was an English horse and I was delighted when we won the Open Intermediate despite the fact I only rode him for the first time about an hour before the dressage. The following week we also led the dressage at the three-day event but everything came to a halt on the cross-country when we had a run out at a bounce combination which dropped us well down the order.

'In the show-jumping the last combination was very unusual and included an upright onto a bank, a stride to a viaduct wall and one stride over an upright off the bank and a big drop off. I was very surprised it didn't cause much trouble but the show-jumping did provide a fitting climax to the event. I finished 14th with Robin Hood which was very pleasing and the whole trip was a fantastic experience as it included a trip to the incredible Grand Canyon and I also had my first ride in a hot air balloon.'

Travelling out to Gawler in Australia for the World Championships in 1986 was an experience Ian will never forget as it didn't exactly go to plan. For a number of reasons he missed the plane and when he finally arrived in Melbourne there was nobody at the airport to meet them and they had no real idea of where they were. Luckily Mark Todd arrived on the scene and when a car arrived to pick him up Ian was given a lift. During the event Ian and Oxford Blue slipped on landing over a fence on the cross-country and saw their hopes of a championship win fade away. The fall pushed Ian and Oxford Blue down to 11th individually.

Ian's first trip abroad with Murphy came at Boekelo in Holland in 1988. Because Ian was in the Olympic team in Seoul he had no chance of schooling Murphy for about six weeks but fortunately Daniel Hughes and Douglas Edward, who were both working for Ian, had kept him fit while he was away. It was five years since Ian had last been out to Holland and with his relatively new partnership with Murphy he was keen to see how they would get on. 'I had last ridden Oxford Blue out there and I knew Murphy would be quite a different ride,' recalls Ian. 'We decided to make it a family holiday as the Dutch hospitality is always excellent and Stephanie and Tim were on holiday from school at the time. Iain Couttie helped out with the driving to the event and we decided we would fly to Amsterdam from Newcastle as a special treat. As is so often the case I was late for the event and arrived just in time for the vet's inspection. Murphy pulled my arms out in the trot-up so I knew he was feeling well.

'He was quite naughty in the dressage and then during the cross-country I managed to fall off on the flat between fences. I flew right over his head and the string at the side of the course. Unfortunately there weren't any spectators there at the time to help me get back on. Somehow we managed to keep the lead as we hadn't lost too much time and he then show-jumped well to hold on to the top position.'

In 1989 Ian took Mrs Reddihough's little horse Foxy V out to the Luhmuhlen three-day event in Germany. Lying fifth and best of the British after the dressage, Jenny and the horse's owner finally made it out to the event for the cross-country after a stressful journey travelling to the event. Recalls Jenny: 'We had hoped to see Ian's dressage but everything seemed to be against us. Foxy V was one of the less experienced horses in the yard when we took him to Luhmuhlen and when we walked the cross-country the going changed from good to very hard within a few feet. The deep, soft sand in places was tiring on the horses' legs and I couldn't see a lot of difference between the course and that used for the 1987 European Championships when we had Sir Wattie who was far more experienced.

'The cross-country began early on the Saturday morning in very hot weather. Ian set off on Phase A in blistering heat. Foxy V did very well to complete without any jumping penalties and although Ian was down on the time we were very pleased with his effort. I was extremely worried about how tired Ian would feel after his round as he was still recovering from a fall, but the great thing was that the comparatively inexperienced horse had gone as well as he had. In 14th place before the show-jumping, Foxy's mark was in the middle of some very close scores.

'The final day promised to be a most interesting one. Overnight rain had softened the ground slightly but the show-jumps themselves seemed enormous. Like the cross-country there was little or no difference to what had been set up for the European Championships two years earlier and it was hardly surprising when Foxy V dropped down to 23rd place. It was disappointing for his owner and Ian but the horse had shown he was capable on the cross-country.

'A few months later and Foxy V rolled out of the yard again this time heading for Melbourne, Australia where he was to compete at Werribee. Ian had been invited to take a horse out there along with Lorna Clarke and Lucinda Green and it seemed too good an opportunity to miss. I had to stay at home because of slipped discs and then while Ian was away one of the students wrote off my three-week old car. Every time Ian rang I was about to tell him and then decided it wasn't a good idea.

'Foxy V arrived safely but I started to get a little worried when Ian rang to say the cross-country course was horrific and eight jumps had to be altered after complaints. When I heard Ian had come home safe I was very relieved. He had gone quite slowly but I wasn't too concerned about that and he was still lying in second place. Three fences fell and Ian thought he would drop well down but after the leader also hit three fences and was slower Ian won. It was a very successful competition despite problems caused by quarantine regulations and the travel arrangements to reach Australia.'

The World Equestrian Games in Stockholm in 1990 brought further success for Ian this time with Murphy who claimed both individual and team silvers. It was a trip Jenny and Ian will never forget. Gold just eluded them by a fraction but Murphy's cross-country was one of the most excitable rides Ian had ever experienced.

'Just to go to Stockholm after everything that had happened that year, was like a dream,' explains Jenny. 'When we arrived home a good friend of ours had decorated the yard with balloons and streamers and a great big poster saying "Murphy Rules OK", to celebrate our return. We felt quite guilty when we arrived home after such an exciting trip and had a dreadful sense of anti-climax as we turned into the drive. I always think it must be an awful moment for our welcome home party when they see our high spirits evaporating like steam as we fall in a heap in front of the television.

'Ian and Murphy bouncing through the road crossing was quite something and has become an eventing legend and Ian watched it time and time again on the video. The way Murphy tackled that enormous fence made us wonder

Ian winning Punchestown on Glenburnie

whether he had been a kangaroo in a previous life.'

With no ride at Badminton in 1993 Ian was in quite a depressed state as the event approached. Fortunately Stanwick Ghost, who was then a seven-year-old, came to the rescue and was going from strength to strength when he finished second at Saumur in France much to Ian's delight. A chequered spring of ups and downs is the only way to describe the first few months of the season and the good result at Saumur lifted Ian's morale.

'When we left for our French trip we hoped we weren't taking out a horse which was too young and inexperienced,' says Jenny. 'Stanwick Ghost had shown he was in good form and was going better and better. The dressage arenas surrounded by pot plants, the twisting cross-country track through woods and the awe-inspiring show-jumping with the accompaniment of a band of French horns did not worry him in the slightest.

'He remained as cool as a cucumber throughout the event and was never off his food for a second which is how he has continued through the whole of his career. We had such a hassle-free event out in Saumur that I was quite glad

Winning at Berrima, Australia, on Volatile (Jenny Stark)

Ian was not rushing back to Badminton. For once we had some time to prepare for Clan Royal going out to Punchestown where he finished a creditable eighth much to Ian's and Lord and Lady Vestey's delight.

'Ruth Day, the Vesteys' head girl, very kindly came to Punchestown to look after Clan Royal. Being there brought back a lot of memories of the European Championships with Glenburnie in 1991. Clan Royal was nothing like as experienced as Glen so we were thrilled with the way he tackled the course in Ireland. Many of the fences were almost the same as two years before.

'His inexperience showed in the dressage and show-jumping where he had two fences down but we were all very pleased. Going out to Ireland for a week can seem quite a long time. But when we had a blow-out on the lorry just north of Dublin that added to the length of the journey home and I think Ian was pleased I had suggested he fly home to ride some more horses.'

· · ·

Over the years Ian and Jenny have had some wonderful times travelling the world as Jenny recalls: 'For a couple of years Ian visited Jamaica to teach and compete and I went with him. We have been to Poland when Ian and Sir Wattie competed at Bialy Bor and for the last few seasons we have regularly visited Australia and New Zealand. Although hectic, they have been fantastic experiences and eventing has taken us to places we wouldn't have been able to visit otherwise.'

Jenny Stark – Wife, Mother and Key Player

'She is completely the lynchpin of the team and Ian relies on her 100 per cent. If you notice at a three-day event, Jenny is always the person who gives him a leg-up. She is a tremendous help and wonderful pair of eyes. I think she should get an MBE.'

BARBARA SLANE FLEMING, IAN'S LONGSTANDING

DRESSAGE TRAINER

Jenny Stark is one of the unsung heroines of the sport of horse trials. A wife, mother, cook and groom all rolled into one, she has been the backbone of the family's great success over the years. Born into a farming family, she grew up surrounded by horses and was taught the rudiments of riding by her mother Jean McAulay, a well respected trainer in the Galashiels area. Jenny started to ride at an early age and when she was 20 years old set up a riding school at her parents' home, Dryden. She has a sister Catriona who now runs the riding school and brother Alistair who farms nearby.

Ian and Jenny met when he started to get help from Mrs McAulay who was training the Ettrick Forest Riding Club team, of which Ian was a member. Gradually their relationship developed and they would meet for mid-day dates, the evenings being out of the question as they were both so busy. Eventually in November 1979, they married and made their home at Haughhead where they have remained ever since.

Jenny inherited her mother's talent for working with young horses and competed in riding club events. By the time they married Ian was gradually becoming known in Scottish eventing circles and gaining a good reputation as

Jenny Stark - wife, mother and key player
(Tim Smith)

a producer and trainer of young horses. Even for Ian, though, it might not have been possible without Jenny's wholehearted support and encouragement.

Jenny has always had a love for Highland ponies and when they married she took six with her to their new home. These were quickly backed, ridden away and sold before their unruly behaviour got too much for Ian but over the years she has managed to sneak one or two ponies into the stables. One of Jenny's favourites was the Connemara stallion Smokey Shane that belonged to Ann Wilson and which she rode in the mid '80s. One Christmas Ian really surprised Jenny when he secretly bought her a young Connemara gelding known as Toby and kept it well hidden before the day. Ian bought him a few weeks before Christmas while travelling home from a day's hunting. A son of Smokey Shane, Ian's next problem was to keep him a secret but fortunately his near neighbours the Gibsons came to the rescue and when Jenny was presented with Toby she was quite taken aback.

As Ian started to make a name for himself in 1982, Jenny threw all her efforts into helping to establish him in the sport while also caring for Stephanie and Tim. The initial few years with Sir Wattie and Oxford Blue were both hard work and exciting as Ian rapidly climbed the horse trials ladder, winning at Bramham with Wattie and then heading for their first Badminton a year later.

The first time Ian competed abroad at Achselschwang in Germany, Jenny remembers it as a long and tiring journey, but it was the first of many travels with the horses. Jenny believes that coming from a horse-orientated background has been an important factor in Ian's success over the years. Her experience has meant she is in tune with his thinking and is the driving force that keeps him going, being able to understand why he is so competitive and the pressures that arise throughout the season.

Haughhead nestles against a hillside below Jenny's mother's farm in the heart of the Scottish lowlands, just off the Carlisle to Edinburgh road. The house has changed somewhat over the years, as trees and old buildings have made way for new stables and a barn. At the time Mrs McAulay was none too keen when the bulldozer came in but in order to develop the yard, changes were needed quite urgently.

Jenny continued to compete for a few years after they were married but she admits that she was never brave enough and decided to take a back seat preferring to run the yard and take charge of the horses' fitness work in the early part of the season. For hour after hour during the cold winter months, Jenny can often be seen riding and leading one of the horses as they set out in preparation to get fit for the spring season after their winter rest. When the stables were full up with 14 horses or more the only way to get them all ridden was to ride and lead and Jenny has continued to do so ever since. During the days of the two grey boys, Jenny would ride Glenburnie and lead Murphy while latterly she has ridden Arakai and led Stanwick Ghost on those cold, wintry mornings. When not in work all horses return home to their owners, giving Ian and Jenny some breathing space at the latter end of the year.

Over the years the white cottage at the side of the road has seen many horses and countless students, working pupils, grooms and helpers come and go. During Glenburnie and Murphy's heyday Haughhead was home to a number of working pupils keen to learn from Ian's experience and everyone was expected to help out at whatever job needed doing. 'Ian has spent endless hours in the school teaching working pupils and the house for a number of years was always overflowing,' says Jenny. 'Stephanie and Tim never knew who would be coming and going next, there were always so many people about. When the house was so full every now and again Ian would get really annoyed about the mess but there was little anyone could do with so many people about. Ian is a real perfectionist who likes everything done properly. He will seem quite a relaxed person to those who don't know him but with the horses

Ian and Jenny, Auchinleck, 1997 (Tim Smith)

he is very organised and systematic. By nature he doesn't like routine but does expect the yard to be tidy.'

In deciding to take on the role of anchorman, it is Jenny who is left in the ten-minute box at the major championships and she can often be seen 'talking to the grass' as Ian gallops from one huge fence to the next. In recent years Lord Hartington has given his support to Jenny on such occasions as she listens carefully to the commentator. It is a time that has never become any easier despite Ian's illustrious career and whenever a spell goes without Ian being mentioned her face becomes more anxious by the minute.

'I have always preferred the one-day events,' says Jenny. 'They are not so intense and a three-day takes up a whole week and can be quite stressful for everyone. Sometimes at a three-day event I may not go until the day before the cross-country so that I can stay at home and keep everything going there.'

Jenny's calming influence and straight forward approach to solving problems has helped keep the team in action. On one of the rare occasions when Jenny wasn't around Ian almost missed his dressage at Burghley in 1986 when riding a young Glenburnie. Jenny arrived after the dressage to be told that Ian had nearly been eliminated for missing his test and had to canter from the stable to the arena before Lucinda Green snatched Glen's tail bandage and they were straight in for their test. In hindsight the last minute dash failed to upset proceedings as Ian and Glen finished a creditable fourth despite coming home with almost a minute to spare on the cross-country.

For Jenny 1988 will always be a special year when Ian finished first and second at Badminton. Ever since Jenny married Ian, she has had to be able to slot into different jobs and get used to him wanting everything done yesterday. In every top event yard there is a 'Jack of all Trades' and it is this role which Jenny has fulfilled successfully throughout Ian's career. Slotting into different roles from lorry driver to cook, practice fence helper to safety girth checker, Jenny is always on hand trying to make sure everything runs harmoniously. Most top event riders agree that to be successful you must have a good back-up team and it is often the case that when that back-up team falls apart so do the consistency and results.

Leading such a hectic life it is inevitable that there have been many times when Ian and Jenny have arrived at functions and events late despite Ian's ability to drive at astonishing speed. 'One evening we were driving to Liverpool for a dinner wondering how on earth we were going to make it on time or if we would make it at all when we suddenly spotted flashing blue lights,' says Jenny. 'I was just beginning to wonder how many more points Ian would get on his licence when we realised we had been stopped because Ian had his fog light on and we both breathed a huge sigh of relief.

'There have been many occasions when we have arrived at an event and forgotten some vital piece of equipment but one of the funniest days was when Douglas Edward was working for us. Ian was wearing a neck brace after a fall but he still decided he wanted to go to an event to help Douglas. I knew something would go wrong, it was just one of those days. Ian was lying down in the back of the lorry not feeling particularly well and when we arrived Douglas realised he had forgotten his jodhpurs. Ian was very annoyed and getting angry was doing his condition no good at all so Douglas was promptly sent off to the second hand clothing stall to buy a pair of jodhpurs. The only ones he could get were ladies and they didn't exactly fit very well but it cheered everyone up when we saw him in them.'

At Lincoln, 1997 (Tim Smith)

Dogs have always been a prominent feature of life at Haughhead and Jenny recalls the day when Sandy the Labrador ran off with one of Stephanie's gloves when she was quite small. 'When Sandy pinched her glove I ran after it to try and retrieve the glove before it was chewed to pieces. Throwing myself at Sandy in rugby tackle style I managed to break the poor dog's leg. Ian wasn't about so I had to ring my brother Alistair who rather grudgingly took me, the dog and the two kids in his tiny sports car to the vet; we must have looked quite a sight squashed into the car.

'Lottie, our Rhodesian Ridgeback whom we got from Charlotte Steel, has got into a number of scrapes when we have taken her to events. At Bramham in 1996 we were fortunate enough to be staying in the house and left Chris Smith, an Australian who was working for us, in charge of the dog. Lottie kept wandering off and when the stable manager announced that the owner of a Rhodesian Ridgeback should collect it from the stables Chris told him he

Before the show-jumping, Badminton 1989. Ian riding Glenburnie and leading Murphy Himself
(*Liz Rhys-Jones*)

(*ABOVE*): The European gold medal team, Burghley 1989. (*left to right*) Rodney Powell (hidden from view), Ginny Leng, Lorna Clarke, Ian on Glenburnie (*Hugo Czerny*)

(*LEFT*): Ian on Murphy and Stephanie on Timpani Drum take part in the Selkirk Common Riding

(*ABOVE*): The team at Belton Park, spring 1997. (*left to right*) Stanwick Ghost, Lady Hartington, Ian, Lady Vestey, Stephanie, Vicky, Jenny, Arakai
(*David Haver*)

(*RIGHT*): Lady Vestey with Arakai in front of Badminton House
(*Lady Hartington*)

Badminton 1997 (*RIGHT*): A delighted Ian leaves the dressage arena on Stanwick Ghost after going into the lead (*Iain Burns*)

(*BELOW*): Safely over the second fence on the cross-country (*Tim Smith*)

(*LEFT*): The final parade before the show-jumping. Ian had maintained his position in the lead after the cross-country
(*Iain Burns*)

(*BELOW*): The picture that says it all . . . leaving the arena after the show-jumping phase
(*Iain Burns*)

(*LEFT*): Jenny at Haughhead on Arakai and leading Mr Mackinnon

(*BELOW*): Stephanie in the tackroom at Haughhead where the names of some of the stable stars can be seen on the walls (*Expo Life*)

The European Championships Burghley 1997. (*ABOVE*) Ian and Arakai warm-up for the show-jumping phase
(*Tim Smith*)
(*BELOW*) The victorious team (*left to right*) William Fox-Pitt, Mary King, Ian, Chris Bartle (*Tim Smith*)

At home with Stanwick Ghost and Lottie, the Rhodesian Ridgeback (*Expo Life*)

didn't want it and it could stay with him. Another time at Blair I had arrived while the dressage was going on to see Lottie heading straight for the arenas and about to cause chaos. Luckily someone caught her and the steward told us we had to pay £10 for the dog causing a nuisance. Waiting outside the lorry Ian eventually paid and we had some trophies that needed returning to the secretary so I politely asked him if he could take those back for us on his way.'

Noodles, the Starks' other dog, arrived after Ian wanted a Doberman. Jenny told him under no circumstances could he have one and when Ian suggested a Rottweiler instead Jenny compromised by allowing Ian to have a black and tan Jack Russell from Tiny Clapham that they called Haggis. The same colour but somewhat smaller than a Doberman, Haggis had pups, and one of the offspring was Noodles who remains not wholly popular with Ian.

After 19 years of marriage, Jenny, is more than used to providing the stability that her family requires and taking the rough with the smooth. All the family realise they are fortunate to have some very good owners and supporters who enable the activity at Haughhead to continue. But this might not have been so if Jenny's temperament had been more volatile and less patient in dealing with the more difficult owners. One rare occasion when Jenny's easy going nature snapped was while travelling home from Punchestown in 1997. The lorries were parked extremely close together on the ferry and as Jenny was walking alongside their own lorry another driver decided he could get past nearly squashing Jenny in the process and damaging the cab door. Everyone in the horsebox watched in amazement as a usually calm and collected Mrs Stark ran after the lorry screaming abuse while Ian remarked that the bloody woman was trying to get herself killed!

Says Jenny: 'I very rarely wish we had done something else with our lives. Maybe I should have carried on competing but it would have proved very difficult with the children and I'm not too sure how Ian would have coped with a competitive wife. Whenever I did ride competitively in the first few years of our marriage, I would come back thinking I had done really well. Then I would tell Ian I had one stop and he would get so annoyed. I love all the preparations before the season, getting the horses fit and the many hours of slow work which pays off in the long run.'

Jenny's preparations for a major event usually start weeks in advance with the horses being mentally as well as physically prepared. She keeps a close eye on Ian's many engagements and aims to have his diary clear of any commitments so that he is free to concentrate one hundred per cent on the events. All too often distractions come along and everyone has to be single-minded in their approach. 'There are always worries with the horses and this will never change but the more free of upsets we are the better. Ian keeps busy and as the years have progressed he spends more and more time working on his own fitness to make sure he doesn't let the horses down.'

There have been many stressful occasions in the run-up to events and the days before Badminton 1996 were quite fraught. Ian and Jenny thought everything was going well with Stanwick Ghost and Mr Mackinnon in top form. But, as often happens tragedy struck when Mr Mackinnon damaged his tendon and Stanwick Ghost had to have one of his shoes removed as he was unlevel. Ian had been slightly concerned about Mackinnon's legs in the build-up work but the vet had said to carry on as he couldn't find any signs of aggravation. So after a final work out with both horses, Ian headed off for Bicton Horse Trials in Devon with Sir Marcus and Forest Glen. He continued to be worried about his two Badminton mounts all weekend and on his return his intuition proved correct. There was Duncan, his legs obviously not in the best of shape and Jack minus a shoe, the farrier, Bernie Tidmarsh being brought in to take a look after he became unlevel. Duncan's tweaked tendon put him out of action for over a year and Jack's shoe was not replaced until they arrived at Badminton, due to a bruise in his foot.

Jenny's role over the years has been to 'keep everything going' and she has always taken full responsibility for the stable routine and making sure the yard runs as smoothly as possible. She also keeps a close eye on the finances in a bid to keep everything afloat while also fending off the bank manager. Jenny recalls with a smile an incident which happened just as she was about to leave for the Olympics in Los Angeles. She had taken Stephanie and Tim to Ian's mother's and said all the necessary goodbyes when the telephone rang. At the other end the bank manager was informing her that the account was very overdrawn and suggesting she shouldn't write any more cheques. 'I couldn't believe it,' she says. 'There I was about to fly to Los Angeles and the bank manager was telling me we had no money, I laugh about it now but at the time it was far from amusing.'

The daily routine at Haughhead can vary but ideally Ian likes to have all the horses ridden by lunchtime leaving the rest of the day free for teaching and other engagements. Jenny likes all the horses to be given quite a lot of

Jenny (right) *on Timpani Drum and Stephanie on Randolph Place return from exercise*

breathing space throughout the day and is not one to fuss over them once they have been finished. Both Jenny and Ian are advocates of low maintenance feeding, believing that many event horses are already too full of beans and on their toes without being fed huge quantities of oats and other high energy feeds. 'There was a time when we fed four times a day but decided to cut down to three with the late feed at 10 p.m. being stopped. We felt it was unnecessary and just caused more work while interfering with the horses, often when they were settled for the evening. The horses receive hay ad lib and Ian is adamant that the hay is very good quality.'

Jenny says the seasons seem to be going quicker and quicker and while she is always ready for a rest over the winter, spring and the fitness work is there before she knows it. She looks upon the winter months as a time when she can take stock of how the season has gone and what needs to be done before they start travelling around the country again. This could mean searching for new horses or having the lorry thoroughly checked over to keep it on the road, carrying out maintenance work at Haughhead or taking a holiday.

When Ian and Jenny started to get busier with Oxford Blue and Sir Wattie she had check lists everywhere to make sure nothing was forgotten but gradually this method was scaled down. The horse trials scene is an extremely friendly circle of people and on the odd occasions when they have forgotten a piece of tack there has always been someone to lend the item. At Belton one year they managed to let all the water out of the tank on the lorry after someone had been to the loo and left the pump on and buckets had to be borrowed to fetch and carry water. Although they have been lucky with the lorry on the whole, one year at Thirlestane, Ruth Day, who was grooming summoned help when she couldn't get the lorry going. Ian was called away from a party in a foul mood only to find the lorry wouldn't start because it was in gear and he had more than a few choice words to say.

All the horses working towards a spring event are brought in at the beginning of January when they start their slow work, walking round the hills that surround Haughhead. As in most top yards once the horses start back in work they will go through a process of clipping, shoeing, worming and having their manes and tails pulled and trimmed. Being based in the Scottish Borders, Ian likes to keep some of the horses' coat on and will often give them a trace clip or blanket clip for the early weeks of their work before they are clipped out fully nearer to the first event. Surrounded by rolling hills and moorland, ideal for when the horses start their fast work, Jenny remains as committed and keen as ever to making sure the horses are brought back into work correctly after their winter rests.

Ian and Jenny like all their horses to return home to their owners during rest periods and horses are often started back on the road to fitness while they are there, Lady Hartington, Stanwick Ghost's owner being especially keen. It will take about 12 weeks to get a horse fit for its first one-day event and 18 weeks for the build up to a three-day.

Once the first few weeks of walking and trotting are underway Ian begins his schooling process. For the more experienced horses it is often just a case of refreshing their memories of work on the flat. The young horses will follow a similar pattern, but at a much slower pace and Ian is insistent that they do not go on to the next stage until the horse clearly understands what is required.

There is little need to get the horses fit by galloping and then walking for set periods of time to build up stamina, instead Jenny relies on the natural gallops around their home on which they have been training for years and know so well. Both Jenny and Ian know how long it should take for a horse to gallop the stretch of land used, how long it should take for them to recover and when they are starting to get fitter. Thanks to this tried and trusted method, the horses are usually just about right for their first event of the season and it is then a question of maintaining this level.

The fast work programme adopted is very similar to that used by racehorse trainers. The horses are cantered every fourth day at no more than a three-quarter-speed gallop. The speed and distance will all depend on the horse being worked and the stage of fitness it has reached.

In her role as fittening expert Jenny also plays a part in Ian's fitness campaign in the run up to the season. When the stables were full to maximum Ian kept fit simply by riding but as the team has gradually been fine tuned he now runs three miles a day as Badminton approaches in the spring. Having his

Giving Ian a leg-up at Badminton (Tim Smith)

own style of training Ian runs as far as he can one way and then waits for Jenny to pick him up in the car. 'I find it too boring to run home along the same track you have just covered,' he declares.

A well-qualified vet is an essential part of the back-up team and when at home in the Borders Ian calls on the services of Reed, Brown and Cameron just a few miles down the road at St Boswells. Says Jenny: 'The head chap, John Reed, dreads coming out to Haughhead. He is never sure what he is going to face and always ends up feeling Ian doubts his professional judgement. When we are in the south we use Geoffrey Brain and Partners who have been the Vesteys' vet for many years and now Charlotte Bathe's husband Andy is so involved with the British team we often contact him for advice. Another key member of the team is the farrier who can mean the difference between success and failure. Elliot Hook has been their blacksmith at Haughhead for nearly ten years while Bernie Tidmarsh shoes the horses while in the south.

Stephanie is full of praise for both Ian and Jenny who have taken on a variety of roles throughout her riding career. Although she turns to Ian for guidance and inspiration she knows that it is Jenny who will be there for both the good and bad times. It is generally agreed that both Ian and Stephanie lean on Jenny for support and after long days at events it is often Jenny who climbs into the driver's seat of the lorry to take them back up to Scotland.

Far from being the over-ambitious mother wanting to produce two more top-level riders, Jenny never actually encouraged Stephanie or Tim to ride. And she soon became an expert on handling people who started to lecture her on why Tim should ride and how important it was that she encouraged him to get into the saddle.

Whenever anyone talks of Jenny it is always in the highest regard. From owner to neighbour and longstanding friends, they all respect the role she has played in the yard's success. In recent years Jenny has seen Stephanie become more and more involved in eventing, progressing from Pony Club to be part of the British Junior team at the European Championships at Blair Castle in 1996. This interest has turned the tables on Ian who is now experiencing some of the stomach churning that Jenny has experienced as he waits for Stephanie to return from the cross-country. 'At last Ian knows what it feels like to be a nervous spectator listening to the commentator. For so many years Ian has been the reason why the rest of us are on tenterhooks and looking so nervous. Now it's his turn,' says Jenny.

$$\left(\,7\,\right)$$

Like Father, Like Daughter
— Like Mother, Like Son

'I was fed up with being called Ian Stark's daughter. At Gatcombe one year I asked Mike Tucker to announce, "And here we have Ian Stark, father of Junior European gold medallist Stephanie," luckily everyone saw the funny side.'

STEPHANIE STARK

An asthmatic since childhood, Stephanie Stark grew up surrounded by horses and success. Taking up riding it was inevitable she would gain the tag 'Ian Stark's daughter' and also face much pressure from her contemporaries. It is never easy for anyone's offspring to jump into the spotlight and follow in either their father's or mother's footsteps.

Just 14 months separate Stephanie and her younger brother Tim, the 'practical and sensible' one who has never taken a great deal of interest in riding preferring the speed and thrill of motor-biking. Not wanting to push either of them into riding both Ian and Jenny recognised that competing at the top-level in eventing was always going to put a lot of pressure on Stephanie.

From the very beginning Ian and Jenny decided the children would be allowed to make their own decisions on whether or not to ride and compete. Stephanie had a number of ponies to ride over the years including Sugar and Foxy who taught her the basics and got her off to a good start. She also started hunting fairly regularly on Charlie a pony owned by Barbara Slane Fleming. On one occasion when out hunting everyone had returned to the lorry to get boxed up to go home. Stephanie dismounted and before she knew

Mother and son: Jenny and Tim at Auchinleck (Tim Smith)

it the pony trotted off and disappeared over the horizon. At first no one thought he would go far but when Ian eventually caught him he had covered quite some distance, only stopping to eat grass on Lord Polwarth's lawn, just beside the Christmas tree covered in lights. Ian dragged him all the way back only for him to pull away again leaving Stephanie squashed against a bank.

Tim is adamant he has not missed out on time with Ian and Jenny but he did sometimes struggle to cope with the discipline when left with Jenny's mother. 'I've never really known any difference and it was my decision not to ride,' says Tim. 'Going out to the Olympics in Atlanta was great fun and everyone especially Stephanie will remember Blair Castle in 1996. She was in the British junior team and the night before her cross-country I kept her awake by being rather ill which didn't go down too well. I very rarely get on a horse but on one occasion at Stowell Park I agreed to ride Stephanie's team horse Go Bust round the polo field. Suddenly I was galloping out of control heading straight towards a wall with Stephanie in hysterics.'

Stephanie and Tim's relationship is similar to that of most brothers and sisters with arguments erupting occasionally but both remain supportive of each others endeavours and Tim is very aware of the pressure Stephanie faces at competitions. As a child he enjoyed the visits to Stowell Park and the freedom that came with them, but now well into his teenage years, Tim prefers to stay at home and carry out any jobs that need doing around the yard.

For Tim the highlight of Ian's career was winning the European Championships at Punchestown with Glenburnie. He remembers the atmosphere as being quite incredible and so different from many of Ian's major wins. At an early age Tim decided he wanted to board at school and took it upon himself to find a suitable establishment, choosing Rannoch School in Perthshire after looking at three schools and says he enjoyed his years there and the freedom that being away from home gave him. 'I have seen the pressure that Dad has been under when competing and never felt it was something I wanted to go through,' says Tim. 'Mum keeps everything going and helps to keep Dad sane when he becomes stressed. She drives the lorry a lot of the time to give Dad a break and the whole set up at home has to be a team effort in order for it to work.'

Remembering his own and Stephanie's early visits to Badminton, Tim recalls the train journeys they undertook to the event with the school secretary on hand to escort them. Once at Badminton, Tim would take off on his bike to tour the trade stands and make a quick stop at the joke shop to arm himself with enough ammunition to last the four days. Throughout their involvement in top-level eventing Ian and Jenny have always been conscious that Tim who was 16 in 1997, is non-horsey and has had to spend a big part of his life at competitions and with people who are very enthusiastic about the sport.

With Ian away competing so much Stephanie was often left to her own devices. But once old enough to ride horses she then started to become more and more interested and evented a little horse for Mrs Knight, Lady Vestey's mother, called Sandy Loch who took her through novices before Lady Howick's Go Bust arrived on the scene. In 1996 she formed part of the gold medal-winning team at the Junior European Championships at Blair Castle with Go Bust. A wonderful occasion but one blighted by a fall at the water on the cross-country. This left Stephanie, in typical Stark fashion, with serious doubts as to whether she deserved the gold medal presented at the end of the event.

When she secured the ride on Go Bust he already knew his job well and was the ideal candidate to give her some experience over larger tracks. Not the easiest of rides and often very strong he means a great deal to Stephanie and is a firm favourite despite his ability to be boisterous and pull free at events to go cantering round the lorry park. Another ride for Stephanie followed in the form of her mother's Lord Patrick, purchased from Gorsebridge as a three-year-old and named after the former British *chef d'equipe* Lord Patrick Beresford. The team's chef at Bialy Bor in Poland in 1986, when Ian was part of the winning team with Sir Wattie, Lord Patrick Beresford played a key role as *chef d'equipe* on a number of occasions during Ian's first few years at the top. Purchased while Jenny and Ian were on holiday, Lord Patrick caught their eye while he was being loose jumped over a pole. Supposed to be having a rest, Ian and Jenny couldn't resist a visit to the sales. Jumping a huge fence, Patrick knocked it down and the show jumpers lost interest. But the next time he came round, the little horse standing no more than 15.2 hands gave the fence a foot and up went Ian's hand.

The stables at Haughhead are more often than not filled with horses belonging to some of Ian's first owners from the early 1980s. Sir Wattie's owner Dame Jean Maxwell-Scott from Abbotsford sent Stephanie Douce

Father and daughter: Ian on Sir Marcus and Stephanie on Go Bust (Expo Life)

Davie to ride for 1997 and Mrs Knight sent Dewpond, a daughter of Sandy Loch. Stephanie had evented Sandy Loch at area Pony Club level and in Junior Regional Novices and she had high hopes for both new arrivals. Combining school with life on the eventing circuit is difficult for any rider and Stephanie admits juggling school commitments and competing leads to a hectic life. 'In 1996 I had major exams to fit around Junior Open Intermediates and Windsor which was very difficult. During the holidays I was supposed to be revising for six hours a day but instead I always seemed to be travelling, riding and worrying about my first Junior Open Intermediate Trial at Belton.

'I remember for my second JOIT at Bicton I hadn't ridden for a fortnight and flew down from school to compete, so I felt totally out of practice and unfit. Then my exams started so I spent my entire exam leave getting ready for Windsor. On the Wednesday of Windsor I had my French exam so I flew down after that and rode Buster at 8 p.m. I was so excited I could hardly sit in my seat during the exam never mind answer questions in French.

'It was much easier preparing for Blair because I had summer holidays, but having to go back to school after that was a real let down. Thankfully my school has always been very understanding and they gave me my school "colours" for riding at the end of the year.'

Coping as the daughter of an international event rider is something Stephanie has come to live with from an early age. 'It is a lot of pressure but I manage. Ever since I was little I've had pressures from other parents but I suppose that gave me more drive as they made me determined to do well. Everyone expected me to win everything because Dad trained me, but really he was always too busy to help me a great deal. Then when I fell off and came last – as I did most of the time – people would wonder what was wrong with me.

'I suppose I've always felt I had something to prove and I wanted to get rid of the label "Ian Stark's daughter" and be successful in my own right. It has helped me to cope with the people in eventing and all the ups and downs. I do feel I'm under pressure to perform well and live up to my Dad's reputation. Some people like to put me down if I don't win or do well at an event, but I suppose if I can cope with that kind of pressure, I can cope with anything and it makes me tough.

'I can't remember not being interested in riding. Dad plonked me on a pony before I could walk and the more competing I've done, the more hooked

I've become. Between the age of ten to 13 I had horrible ponies and I seriously thought about giving up but I don't think I could now.'

Ian believes life on the eventing circuit is difficult for Stephanie because so much is expected and she has to work even harder than most. He is both her biggest supporter and biggest critic and during training sessions in the school at home expects Stephanie to ride to her full potential.

During competitions at one-day level Ian usually manages to be around to help out and give advice but when it comes to the three-days and cross-country phase he is often found wandering about nervously listening carefully to the commentary. When Stephanie and Go Bust fell at the Junior Europeans in 1996 Ian says his stomach hit his boots. And even reliving the action on video causes him heartache. Watching Stephanie compete at a higher level has finally made Ian realise what it must be like for Jenny and the rest of the team as they listen to the commentary as he gallops round at Badminton, Burghley and the Olympics.

Highlights of competing together include Royal Deeside where Stephanie took the under 21s trophy and Ian scooped the veterans title. Both Ian and Stephanie are great perfectionists and this can at times lead to arguments and frustrations from both sides. Now and again there are major fall-outs and tears but on reflection both realise this is down to their strong desire to succeed. Keen to praise his daughter on her finer points, Ian believes Stephanie is very good at walking courses and seeing a stride and recognises he can be quite forceful when helping her in the school at home with the young horses. 'She thinks I'm too hard on her but I only want things to be right and for her to succeed,' says Ian. 'Whether I am teaching Stephanie or another pupil, my teaching methods and attitude are the same, high standards at an early stage are important to future success.'

Ian has always ensured that whatever Stephanie has done in connection with riding it has been because she wanted to and not because she is his daughter. 'Eventing has to be fun and you must really want to compete. You can be so uptight with nerves thinking how the course is going to ride or how good your dressage test will be. Sometimes at competitions Stephanie can be really keyed up and emotional, after a dressage test has gone well the relief is enormous for everyone and there are so many highs and lows.'

After a major three-day event both Ian and Stephanie suffer a huge sense of anti-climax after the adrenaline rush which has kept them going throughout. Admits Ian: 'Win or lose, it can be an awful feeling and in the early days after a major championship no one would speak to me for a few days until I had calmed down.'

At competitions Ian recognises that for much of the time Stephanie likes to work on her own without too much pressure. She is already hard enough on herself without others making competition days worse. For many riders the cross-country phase is the section they enjoy most about horse trials but it is also the most worrying. Once her horses are tacked up and ready to go Stephanie will get someone to check her safety girth and then make her way to the start quietly on her own.

During the winter it is often the case that Ian and Stephanie won't see each other for a couple of months as both lead such busy lives and Ian can be away teaching. But having a father who has travelled the world with his chosen sport, Stephanie soon recognised the importance of his being away from home, developing an independent attitude to her riding and relying on Jenny for advice.

A long-term aim is to compete at Badminton alongside her father but Jenny is unsure how she could cope having two riders to calm and organise

Father and son: Ian tests Tim's new bicycle (Tim Smith)

over the four days. To Stephanie Badminton is a major part of the eventing year, but a week that is always full of drama as 1997 proved. 'I always forget what a strain Badminton is. Vicky Welton, our head girl and I commuted from Stowell Park every day so we missed some of the stressful moments, but it was pretty harrowing anyway. Badminton is the ultimate competition, and having two horses there was amazing. I was worried for Arakai who seemed very inexperienced but he seemed very settled throughout the competition and for some reason I was less worried about him on the cross-country than Stanwick Ghost. His stamina and scope meant that he made the course look easy, and he finished with the same look on his face as Lord Gyllene, who shares the same sire, after the Grand National. It was easier coping with Arakai's performance as we put no pressure on him and all our hopes really rested on Stanwick Ghost who we all knew was capable of leading after the dressage.

'This made Saturday a complete nightmare, but at least Arakai's earlier round had filled us with confidence. I stood in the television tent in the ten-minute box willing Stanwick Ghost over every fence and just burst into tears when I saw them come through the finish flags. I was so proud and so relieved that they were back safely. Then we realised that 1996 was happening all over again and I just hoped that Stanwick Ghost wouldn't give us a repeat of his show-jumping performance. To be honest I thought he could win it – it seemed like his year and Dad definitely deserved it.

'I didn't watch his round then and I still haven't seen it, preferring to stand behind a trailer with my fingers in my ears, but I still heard the gasps of the crowds, it was a heartbreaking time and I have never been so disappointed.'

Stephanie's talent is highly regarded by Ian's dressage trainer Barbara Slane Fleming who says: 'She is very much her father's daughter who faces a lot of pressure from the media but not from home. She is very determined, thinks for herself and is very talented. Although she doesn't ride like Ian, she can see a stride a long way out from a fence and I am very impressed with her ability.'

It would appear superstition runs deep in the Stark household, especially where Ian and Stephanie are concerned. Stephanie will no longer allow Ian to fasten her medical armband after falling off at a competition when he checked it. And she also favours purple when bandaging her horses.

Just like her father, Stephanie rides horses for a number of people and she is grateful for their continuous loyalty and support. 'Phoebe Stewart who owned my first horse has been a great inspiration. She has trailed up and down the country to support me – even when I wasn't riding her horse,' says Stephanie.

It was Stephanie's association with Lady Howick's good horse Go Bust that took her to a place in the Junior European team at Blair Castle and she recognises that such rides are so necessary to provide similar opportunities. 'Lady Howick gave me the ride on a brilliant horse at the right time and she is very supportive, always happy even when it all goes out of the window and is an excellent owner.

'I'm unbelievably lucky with my owners and always have been. So far they have all been very undemanding and understanding. Lady Howick has coped with my tears and tantrums and has celebrated with me when things have gone well. Mrs Knight has always been very encouraging and was keen that I rode Dewpond. Dame Jean Maxwell-Scott is no stranger to the role of owner and is very kind and far more concerned that I am enjoying the ride and the horse is well rather than winning prize after prize. Mum and Super Solvitax jointly owned Lord Patrick and the support from the latter has been invaluable. I am very lucky and very grateful to all my owners for their enthusiasm, dedication and generosity and truly appreciate that they do not pressure me. In fact the only owner to ever pressurise me was Phoebe Stewart who, in the nicest possible way offered me money to beat Dad show-jumping.'

When looking for future event stars Stephanie admits she very much has her own opinions on what types she likes and dislikes – and it often differs greatly from her father's. 'This is where our opinions vary,' she laughs. 'He goes for elegant, pure thoroughbreds as he loves their speed and quality and can cope with their temperament. I prefer a slightly chunky, more powerful horse with a real spark about them. The only horse Dad and I can agree on is Stanwick Ghost – he likes his elegance and speed whereas I like his exuberance and naughtiness. He's got real character and I feel that a horse can make up in temperament what it lacks in quality. For that reason Go Bust really suited me. Having said that, I really like the old steeplechaser, powerful type and would have loved to have had the chance to ride Sir Wattie – he was so clever and had real charisma.'

To this day Wattie remains Stephanie's favourite horse to grace the yard at Haughhead. 'He would give his all to Dad and remains one of only a handful of horses that we have had in the yard who you could trust completely to do

Stephanie at home with Go Bust (Expo Life)

his best. I remember doing some cross-country on a naughty pony called Harley while Dad was schooling Wattie. The pony was being so horrible that Dad decided to sort him out, so I got on Wattie and started jumping.

'The horse had never fallen in his entire career but I managed to throw him over a three foot high post and rails. I ended up on the ground and had to be rushed-off to hospital for X-rays. Nevertheless I always enjoyed riding him. Glenburnie and Murphy were both very special and Glen's win at the Europeans in 1991 is the one that sticks in my mind above all the other victories. Hopefully Arakai will be the next star and Stanwick Ghost will always be a favourite despite his show-jumping.'

Nineteen ninety-seven was a busy year for Stephanie with four horses to ride and more time to devote to competing once school was over. After a novice outing with Lord Patrick at Lincoln, Stephanie took Go Bust to Gatcombe where she competed in a stiff Open Intermediate section. 'I was quite lucky to get to Lincoln at all as a French exchange student was staying for the week,' says Stephanie. 'However Dad had already entered Patrick for his first novice and I did everything possible to get there so Dad couldn't have the ride. He did a fairly good test, considering it was his first outing of the season and he felt as if he had grown up.

'At Gatcombe I thought Buster could have gone better in the dressage but Dad said he had shown some of the best lengthening ever in an arena. After Lincoln I decided to ride Patrick in a martingale for more control and thought I should be stronger with him now that he wasn't such a baby. There was a huge improvement in all three phases with some encouraging comments from the dressage judge.

'Buster was also on form and it was a good sign when he came out feeling fresh and well. It was his first outing so I wasn't expecting an amazing test, but his exuberance meant that we got some excellent marks for our mediums. One pole fell in the show-jumping after he became very strong and after I had finished the cross-country I remembered why I enjoyed riding him so much.'

At Belton Park Horse Trials, Ian spent time with Stephanie and Buster working them in before the dressage and show-jumping phases but for the cross-country he stayed well out of the way. He is very keen for Stephanie to do well but only to the extent where she wants to continue and push herself as far as she feels is right at the time.

At Belton, Buster worked in really well but became quite tense during the test, which left Stephanie quite disappointed. In fact they did receive a very good mark and it was only because Stephanie is a perfectionist that she was left feeling slightly uptight. Again at competitions, where Ian has the time he will work with Stephanie before the show-jumping over the practice fences. He knew just what to do to keep both Stephanie and Buster's confidence and then left them to think for themselves. 'Too much advice, and it only gets too confusing,' says Ian. 'Stephanie knows the horse well and whatever happens outside, it is Stephanie who will have to think for herself once she is in the ring.'

If the show-jumping doesn't go too well both Ian and Jenny will allow everything to calm down and then if Stephanie asks for advice it is readily available. Ever supportive and watchful, Ian and Jenny, were thrilled with the ride Stephanie gave Buster at Belton. Ian had his own bird's eye view with Lady Vestey and Lady Hartington after they received a lift in one of the steward's Range Rovers and followed Stephanie round the course much to her annoyance.

Says Stephanie: 'Belton 1997 did not exactly go to plan. I worked Buster hard during the days leading up to my dressage in the hope that he would not blow up. Unfortunately this tactic didn't work. He was working in beautifully, but as soon as we got in the arena he became tense and tanked round with very little softness. Thankfully the judge was feeling generous so I was placed second going into the show-jumping, but I remember thinking at that stage I would have preferred to have done a good test rather than be comparing myself with the others. I was really annoyed with Buster but everyone else seemed to think my test was all right so I had to be happy on the outside. But if Dad had ridden a similar test he would have been very annoyed.'

During the spring of that year Stephanie was aiming for another place on the British Junior team with Go Bust, but after a disappointing showing at Punchestown where they had two run-outs on the cross-country, their chance of a place diminished. 'Goring Heath was my last run before Punchestown and I felt slightly under pressure to get things together. I spent much longer working in for my dressage and it seemed to pay off as Buster did his best test of the season at that stage. His previous two dressage tests had been tense and strong so I was pleased at how relaxed he was. I was very nervous about the show-jumping having mucked up at Belton and my worries were fairly obvious.

'I rode like a complete idiot – hooked and missed my stride at every fence and nearly fell off in the middle of the combination. Somehow I managed to get away with one pole down but I felt like shooting myself. Needless to say I was worried that I would ride just as badly on the cross-country: if I had I would have had a serious accident.

'I set out with the dubious theory that the faster I rode the less likely I was to miss, but thankfully Buster wasn't paying much attention to me so I let him get on with it. It was quite a difficult track with a big water complex and double of arrowheads so my clear round gave my confidence a much needed boost. To top it all I then discovered I had the same dressage mark as Dad in the same section and he was riding Arakai who was heading for Badminton.'

Stephanie was really excited about Punchestown despite a 12-hour journey with a number of deviations on the way. She had been excused the trials at Windsor due to a clash with exams, to run in Ireland instead. And after trotting up both Buster and Marcus for Ian who was judging the hunters at Windsor, there was plenty of time to relax.

'I didn't do my dressage until Saturday afternoon and Buster was working really well. I thought we did a good test and lots of other people said it was nice, so I was expecting a fairly good mark. Unfortunately Lady Carew wasn't so impressed and instead of being in the low 50s I ended up with a score of 61 which left me fifth. I was fairly cross and Dad looked as if he was about to wring someone's neck, so I went off to do my last course walk with Mum and Lady Howick. The course was lovely – well built, imaginative and inviting so although I was nervous I was hoping for a good ride as I thought the big attacking fences would suit Buster.

'I had a brilliant steeplechase and despite the rain I was more relaxed than usual in the ten-minute box. I really went for it on the cross-country but instead of settling into a fast rhythm I felt Buster getting longer and stronger and by the sixth fence I was having major problems holding him. I couldn't get him back in front of the fences and my steering was fairly non-existent. Eventually I had a run out. The New Grange was the only fence at which I thought I was risking anything by going straight. Like Dad, I don't like taking long routes, so I decided to do the more difficult option which involved jumping a table, taking two strides and jumping on to a huge mound.

'Buster jumped in well but then suddenly ducked to the right. I circled and jumped up a smaller alternative but I was really disappointed. I went on but

Buster felt as if he wasn't really focused on me. We had a strange stop coming out of the last water fence, three from home, and we completed very tired.

'I don't know what went wrong but he'd never felt like that before and I just hoped there was nothing physical bothering him. He was a bit stiff at the trot-up but passed easily and felt fine while warming up for the show-jumping. He jumped well and had just one fence down, despite a hairy moment in the combination, when he went down on his knees but just managed to scrape himself over the last element.

'All in all we finished sixth and despite being a little disappointed I had an excellent time and gained a lot of experience. The highlight of the week however was definitely the stripper we hired for Lucinda Murray's groom, Hannah who was 21 on the Saturday.

'After we returned from Punchestown, Buster went back to Lady Howick for a rest and at the time it was felt that for the autumn we should aim for a couple of Open Intermediates rather than push him too much more. He didn't owe me anything and it wouldn't have been fair to keep trying to do three-day events. But after he returned from Lady Howick's, Buster didn't quite feel the same and when we were starting to get him fit we decided age was catching up with him and he should be retired, having given me so much fun and experience.'

Few young riders are constantly bought advanced horses and with Stephanie's long term prospects in mind following Punchestown she spent much of the year producing novices. Stephanie tried Dewpond the Monday after Badminton and immediately liked the mare, feeling she could aim for a one-star three-day event in the autumn after a couple of novice outings with her previous rider, Caroline Graham.

Douce Davie was an entirely different animal – a horse with plenty of ability he was also very sharp and Ian decided he would event the horse for a couple of outings before Stephanie took over. Two events in the summer saw Stephanie taking Lord Patrick to Oatridge and she followed this up with a visit to Hexham on the Wednesday after Bramham.

'Oatridge was Patrick's first event for a while. We arrived late and I had next to no time to work in, so I had a fairly mediocre dressage test, but fortunately he stayed relaxed despite the stress. He was slightly onward bound in the show-jumping and booted out two poles but I wasn't too annoyed as it was his first outing for weeks. Then I found my "mediocre" test had actually been quite good – that always seems to happen to me. For the first half of the cross-country he felt quite rusty but gradually he settled and I left the event feeling quite optimistic.

'Dad was unable to go to Hexham after his fall at Bramham as he was still very sore and shaken, and to be honest it was quite a relief. It was my first outing with Dewpond so it was nice to be without pressure. Both horses did lovely tests and were marked well, with Patrick being given a 17 and Dewpond 22. I was really pleased as I thought only people like Dad got dressage marks under 20. Unfortunately my show-jumping wasn't so successful. Patrick completely took off with me and had two down, while Dewpond hit four, unable to cope with the wet conditions.

'I forgave her as she had never seen mud like it before, but I was really annoyed with Patrick so I decided to put him in a pelham for the cross-country. This gave me much more control and steering, and I had an amazing cross-country round even jumping an arrowhead which was quite a turn around. I didn't push Sally as the ground was deep but she grew in confidence and we came home with just one stop at the coffin. She gave me an excellent feel so I was thrilled and the day ended well with Patrick finishing seventh, earning his first point.'

Stephanie hadn't expected to be able to ride at Burgie the following week as the novice was originally planned for the Friday, her final day at school and it was a pleasant surprise when the section was moved to Sunday. After a tiring week of end-of-term celebrations she left the partying to the others at Burgie but was still rather disorganised on the Sunday morning. 'For some reason I had left everything to the last minute and a quick trot up to the dressage arena wasn't really enough working in time for Patrick. Needless to say my test wasn't particularly impressive which put Dad in a bad mood and the expression "bear with a sore head" sprang to mind, which was only made worse by a poor test on Dewpond. Thankfully they both show-jumped and went round the cross-country really well, just finishing out of the placings.'

After much discussion it was decided that Ian would ride Douce Davie on his first outing after coming to Haughhead. Quite a difficult horse with a volatile temperament, he showed a lot of talent providing his rider could keep him calm enough during the dressage. Never too keen on letting Ian ride her horses, on this occasion Stephanie had little say in the matter and it was Ian who took the ride at Kincardine O'Neil in the middle of July.

Stephanie on Lord Patrick who was tragically killed in a fall at Hopetoun House in 1997
(Shaw-Shot)

Says Stephanie: 'I'm never great about letting Dad ride my horses and it doesn't happen very often. What really annoys me is they always go better for him and while I can spend weeks working on one problem he can sort it out in five minutes. I find this unbelievably frustrating, and thankfully he understands so only rides my horses if I have a major problem or if I'm not there.

'In Davie's case he wanted to make sure the horse was safe to ride at an event as he could be unpredictable and I found it helpful to know what to expect. Unfortunately I think many people believe Dad is always schooling my horses for me and the comments I get from people never cease to amaze me. The day after Kincardine O'Neil I took Davie to a local riding club combined-training as I knew he would be quiet and manageable. I was only trying to get to know the horse, but as an added bonus we won the competition. Inevitably half the riding club smugly told me with tongues in cheek it was all thanks to Dad schooling Davie the day before.'

Stephanie's team of novices continued to improve with Patrick picking up a place at Auchinleck in Ayrshire when they had an unlucky pole down in the show-jumping and Davie had his first outing. Despite an exciting ride while working in for the dressage once Davie was in the arena he started to concentrate and a good clear show-jumping was followed by a safe cross-country performance which gave the partnership a solid start.

'I love Auchinleck and was especially excited about riding Douce Davie there. I really didn't know what to expect from him and all Dad had said was to be careful warming him up for the show-jumping. Needless to say I got a bit worried when he tried to buck me off several times before we had even gone near a dressage arena. Thankfully he did settle and completed a fairly nice test which was only slightly spoiled by him fidgeting because of the flies, but as soon as we left the arena he was jumping around all over the place. I was a bit apprehensive about the show-jumping, but he actually jumped brilliantly. Despite being excitable he has a lot of natural spring and cleared every fence by about a foot. I was therefore much more relaxed about the cross-country and had a brilliant ride. He felt as if he was really enjoying himself being very bold and sharp.'

Just two days later Stephanie travelled to Cornbury Park horse trials in Oxfordshire with Patrick and Dewpond. Growing in confidence she picked up another place on Patrick, who was going from strength to strength, and cemented her relationship with Dewpond by finishing the event with an enthusiastic cross-country round to delight her owner Mrs Knight who had taken the trouble to go along and support them.

'Cornbury Park was a lovely event and had always been somewhere where I wanted to ride,' says Stephanie. 'I took Dewpond and Patrick down to do the Novice and was pleased to find the course was quite challenging. I knew that if they went well round there both horses would be ready to do an Intermediate. Patrick and Dewpond completed good dressage tests, earning a 24 and a 26. Patrick went on to show-jump really well and was very unlucky to roll one pole but Dewpond didn't jump brilliantly, which was mainly my fault, and had two down. This was a blessing in disguise as I was able to take her slowly on the cross-country and as the course was very technical I was grateful for the opportunity to take time and make sure I got it right. It also gave me the chance to try a new bit, a Dutch gag, which proved very successful. She gave me a lovely ride and Patrick also went brilliantly – he was confident at all the technical fences and found a new, faster gear. We finished with only one time penalty and the round filled me with confidence for my forthcoming Intermediate. He also finished ninth in a very hot section so I was thrilled. Another point!'

After much talk at home Ian and Stephanie felt Patrick was ready to take a step up from Novices and they were entered for the Open Intermediate at Gleneagles. 'I only took Patrick to Gleneagles as it was our first Intermediate and I wanted to be able to concentrate fully on getting it right,' says Stephanie. 'It was also my aunt's wedding on the Saturday night so I thought one horse would be enough to cope with the next day.

'I was fairly confident that Patrick would cope with the jumping elements of the event, but was worried about the dressage. He tends to get very tense and I didn't want the introduction of new movements to completely blow his brain. Even having to do sitting trot throughout the test was going to be a challenge. Thankfully there was no pressure on me so I treated it very light-heartedly and our warm-up consisted of trotting and cantering on a long rein with me bouncing around in the saddle.

'It actually worked very well and Patrick did a very reasonable, if not spectacular, test. We left as soon as I finished to get back home for the wedding but friends of ours rang us in the lorry to tell me the mark. Unfortunately Dad took the message while I was paying for diesel and when I got back he and Vicky took great delight in telling me that I had been given a 48. I was less than happy as I thought the test was all right, so I sat fuming for about ten minutes until I realised that the mark was wrong and Dad and Vicky were in complete hysterics. They seemed to find it funny to add 20 penalties to my real score and I had in fact received a 28 which was well up with the leaders. I was absolutely ecstatic – only a mark behind Arakai – so I proceeded to get very drunk at the wedding which was not a good idea. I woke feeling pretty rough, but thankfully Patrick was jumping out of his skin. We had one show-jump down, and then went on to do an excellent cross-country round.

'Patrick sailed over the fences, and if I had not gone quite so slowly we could have been placed. Unfortunately we were given a technical refusal for crossing our tracks when taking a long route but I still had my qualification for Blair CCI and I knew that Patrick would cope with it. He gave me an amazing feeling which was made even better by the thought that I had brought him to that level and produced him from a complete novice.'

His good round in the Open Intermediate set Patrick up for Blair Castle, which had been the season's aim when suddenly disaster struck. A final run at Hopetoun House near Edinburgh had been going well until they had a crashing fall on the cross-country at a bounce fence near the end of the course. Stephanie was thrown clear of the jump and Patrick died instantly leaving everyone shocked and distressed.

Rushed to hospital with a damaged hand, Stephanie was released after a couple of days and somehow had to come to terms with the tragic loss of a young horse on which she had started to form a real partnership. 'The fall really shook me up. I hurt my hand and broke a tooth, but the worst thing was losing Patrick. I had never lost a horse before and hope I never have to go through it again. I tried to put it to the back of my mind and put a brave face on things. Everyone was really supportive but I should have given myself more time to get over the accident properly. Instead I jumped straight back into the saddle and tried to ride at Ivesley Horse Trials. Being back at a competition really freaked me out and made me realise how serious my accident was and I decided it would be better to take a break from riding for a while.'

Jenny adds: 'This was the first time we had lost a horse in this way for 20 years and it was very upsetting for everyone. Patrick had started to show just

The family at home, summer 1997 (Expo Life)

how talented he was and Stephanie thought such a lot about the horse. Such accidents happen from time to time but however long you have been in the sport the loss never gets any easier.'

The fall left Stephanie with her arm in plaster and time to reflect on how the season had been going while helping out on the yard as much as she could. Douce Davie returned to Dame Jean and Ian took over the ride on Dewpond for the few events that remained.

Stephanie is only too aware of the pressure Ian is under at the major events and for the Open Europeans at Burghley in 1997 she decided it would be better to stay at home. 'It just happened that I wasn't greatly involved with the Open Europeans and when Dad and the team left to go south at the end of August I stayed in the north keeping an eye on things. While they were busy with team training, then Blenheim and Burghley, I was desperately trying to find a job. I didn't go to either of the big three-day events as I knew they would be pretty stressful and any extra people would just be in the way. Instead I made sure no major disasters occurred at home and managed to get myself a part-time job at The Edinburgh Woollen Mill in Jedburgh.

'Funnily enough I also managed to find time to throw a house party on the Friday night of Burghley. It was just as well that Saturday was a success for Dad or I might have been in serious trouble, as by Saturday night my parents seemed to know all about my "little gathering". Thankfully the house wasn't totally trashed although it did take a few days to get the smell of alcohol and cigarettes to fade. And fortunately Mum came back a couple of days ahead of Dad – I don't think my standards would have been good enough for him, but Mum was quite laid back about it all.

'After a fairly disappointing season everyone was completely thrilled about how well Burghley went. It was a fairly last minute decision that Dad was even going to go to the Europeans, and after the final trial everything just seemed to happen really quickly. It was a major bonus that they were chosen for the team but that just increased the pressure that Arakai was under. I was quite worried about him as he seemed so young and inexperienced, but as he had gone so well at Badminton we all knew that he was capable of such a big challenge.

'As it turned out it would have been a waste of time taking him back to "normal" three-star competition. His performance at Burghley proved all the critics wrong and those who said he wasn't ready were made to eat their words. It was very special for the whole team because it brought an amazing end to a pretty awful season. It was also lovely to see Arakai enjoying himself as a star of the future and he was arguably one of the most talented horses competing. Obviously it was a disappointment that he had two show-jumps down and lost the chance of an individual medal, but his time will come and his performance on the Saturday was enough to keep everyone more than happy.'

(8)

Grooming for Scotty

*'There wouldn't be an Ian Stark without his Coca-Cola and chocolate
supply, he wouldn't be able to cope.'*

GROOM VICKY WELTON

Following Ian's decision to quit his full-time job to work with horses the
yard expanded and there was a need to take on staff to help the set-up at
Haughhead run smoothly. One of the first grooms to work for Ian was Claire
Colebrook (née Davies) who joined Ian and Jenny straight from school.

'I used to go for riding lessons at Dryden, which Jenny and her sister ran,'
explains Claire. 'Then when I was 14 my parents bought me a pony from
Jackie Rodgers who Ian was riding for at the time. And once I was old enough
to leave school my father said I was allowed to work with horses for a year
before doing something more constructive.

'At the time I couldn't see past a horse and went to Eglinton Horse Trials
with Ian for a taster to see if I liked it before I started a few weeks later. Most
of the time it was a case of doing whatever was required from looking after
Stephanie and Tim who were quite young then or getting the horses ready for
the events. It was the autumn of 1982 and I remember thinking the job was
wonderful. Although I wasn't the best pupil Ian has ever had, I enjoyed the
riding and had high standards when it came to turnout. I'm not the bravest
rider in the world but when Ian gave me instructions to do something I just
did it. For a while I was running the yard with Jenny and I mucked out enough
stables to last me a lifetime.

'We spent a lot of time taking horses to hunter trials and small events with
Ian leaving instructions which horse he wanted tacked up next and when it

had to be ready. We were always travelling somewhere and seemed to be on the road forever. Bramham was the first three-day event I groomed at and everyone's nerves were a bit frayed by the whole experience. When Ian finished first and third it was incredibly exciting. Jenny and I couldn't believe it and I think we got more out of it than Ian: we thought it was such an achievement whereas Ian was looking to the next step forward and upward.'

Having spent a year with Ian and Jenny, Claire's father suggested she undertake an agricultural secretary's course at a college in Fife but most weekends and whenever they were away competing she stepped in and ran the house and yard for them. 'Following Bramham I groomed for Ian at Badminton in the spring of 1984 and was quite overawed by the whole experience. One of the cross-country jumps near the end of the course had a roof over it and both Ian's horses had never come across anything like that before. Staying at Lorna Clarke's just before the event we put the two horseboxes close together and

Claire Davies riding Glenburnie and leading Kingarth with Jenny behind on Sir Wattie and leading Griffin

draped a tarpaulin between the two to create a roof. We then made a jump out of pallets to test the horses in the hope they would get used to such a fence.

'I felt it was very important that the horses and equipment looked immaculate at Badminton as it was by far the biggest event I had ever been to and with all the official passes we had to have and the marvellous old stables it was quite amazing. All the grooms working at Badminton seem to make that extra effort and when the public used to visit the stables it was very special. Walking the course I couldn't believe how big it was and wondered how on earth the horses would get round. No one dreamed that Ian would do so well at his first Badminton.'

Claire couldn't believe her luck when she was asked if she could go to Los Angeles with Oxford Blue and Sir Wattie for the Olympics. 'The Olympics were a fantastic experience and the first time I had travelled a long way from home. There had been a lot of hype about the event and at team training the army came in to show the grooms how to polish the riders' boots and have everything just spot on.

'We were given a metal box for all the equipment and I thought I would never get everything, including saddles and bridles, in until some of the more experienced grooms showed me it was possible. Ferdi Eilberg, Pat Burgess and Lady Hugh Russell had helped the riders throughout team training at Wylye in Wiltshire before the horses left from Stanstead and we flew from Heathrow. As I was a relatively new groom on the circuit I didn't fly with the horses and had the luxury of sitting back and relaxing on the flight out.

'When the horses came off the plane they had to be washed off with chemicals and spent a few days in quarantine before we were able to get them prepared for the competition. When we had settled in and seen that the horses were comfortable in their stables the next few days meant a lot of early starts but luckily the grooms were staying in dormitories above the stables. Everything was ultra smart for the dressage and Robbie's test went really well.

'During the competition I rode out Wattie who was the reserve horse but I always felt Robbie was the safer one to ride, he was much more of a gentleman whereas I never knew if Wattie was going to put in the odd buck. The horses were such a treat after Ian had been on them and I always enjoyed riding out. For the cross-country we travelled to Fairbanks ranch and had the most horrible ride in one of the lorries – we couldn't see where we were going and it was very hot.

'I walked the cross-country course the day before and was surprised how ornate and beautifully built it was. There was a great team spirit and I was very relieved when Ian and Robbie finished the cross-country safely. Working so close to the horses it is very easy to get attached to them and during every cross-country round I just wanted them to cross the finish line in one piece. We moved back to Santa Anita for the show-jumping and Robbie was very tired. Ian did his best and when the team finished in silver medal position there was a lot of celebrating. A photograph of the grooms leaving the arena with bunches of flowers appeared in *Horse and Hound* and the whole experience was quite incredible.

'When the competition had finished the grooms were taken on some wonderful trips and we had time to unwind before flying home to a big party at Ashkirk Hall. There were so many local people there and they were so excited to see Ian and the horses back. Once the celebrating had quietened down I returned to college but helped out whenever I was needed, fetching Stephanie and Tim from school and looking after the yard when they were away.'

When Claire married her husband Mark in 1989, Stephanie was called on to act as a bridesmaid and she has maintained close links ever since. 'Living at Haughhead for a while, the intense activity does rub off on you and I've never found it easy to sit down for any length of time. We were always unpacking the lorry and re-packing to go to the next event and there was never a dull moment. If we weren't travelling the other job that always needed doing was creosoting the stables.

'I learnt a lot at Haughhead and had some of the best years there. Ian was becoming increasingly well known and it was wonderful as he achieved one ambition after another. Wattie and Robbie were two great horses and with the support of The Edinburgh Woollen Mill it was a real team effort. I was very fortunate to be able to watch Ian work the horses so often – he always appeared so natural in the saddle and I have followed his career throughout.'

• • •

Ruth Day has been Lord and Lady Vestey's head girl for longer than she cares to remember and through her work has known Ian, Jenny, Stephanie and Tim from the first time they visited Stowell Park to see if the estate would be a suitable southern base. Every spring their arrival has brought chaos to her normally organised set up in the stables but she wouldn't have it any other way and is always pleased when she sees the lorry coming up the drive. Working for Ian's longstanding owners and supporters, Ruth's role over the years has involved helping out when an extra pair of hands was needed and assisting the younger grooms with her considerable knowledge. She has groomed twice for Ian at Badminton, in 1990 for Glenburnie and seven years later for Arakai.

Says Ruth: 'When Ian and Jenny first came to look round Stowell Park, no one knew what to expect. Lady Vestey's sister Henrietta Knight had suggested Stowell would be a suitable base and I think they were very impressed with the set-up. It was quickly agreed they would take up the offer and before we knew it they arrived with about ten horses, grooms, children and dogs. I had first heard of Ian when he was third and sixth at Badminton in 1984. I remember the commentator introducing him as the unknown young man from the Scottish Borders but I didn't realise then that the Stark team was going to be such a part of my life at Stowell.'

When they arrived Lady Vestey asked Ruth to help out whenever they needed someone to stand in if they were away competing and she remembers vividly the day Ian had asked her if she could lead one of the horses out for some grass while they were at an event. Doing as she was asked Ruth led the horse out in a head collar and set off for the polo ground at Stowell. As they reached the top of the field the horse gradually became more and more agitated until it eventually took off. Ruth went one way and the horse the other while she was left thinking what a good start the arrangement had made as this valuable horse galloped off into the distance.

During the first few years Ian's horses were based in the top yard and Ruth says the arrangement was fairly hassle free. The team was extremely busy, coming and going to events and a series of lecture demonstrations. These saw the lorry leaving in the early hours of the morning and returning to pick up another load of horses late into the night. When the grey boys, Murphy and Glenburnie, came to the fore as Ian's two top rides the horses moved down to the bottom yard where the stables were bigger and this brought a great deal more activity into Ruth's daily routine. Lord and Lady Vestey had also bought a horse for Ian by this time and for about three seasons the family moved in and shared Ruth's flat.

'I just went with the flow,' laughs Ruth. 'It was much easier to fit in with them and let them take over rather than try and lay down any rules. For a while it was rather squashed with all the students and there were many occasions when the children slept on the settee in the sitting room. Eventually Lord and Lady Vestey suggested Ian and Jenny move into the house and I just shared the flat with the grooms.

'Whenever they come to stay the washing machine is on the go non-stop and gets very little rest until the lorry pulls out of the yard after Badminton. I think the only thing Ian hasn't put in so far is the water buckets. Jenny is an absolute marvel and copes with everything and organises everyone while Ian and I know each other's boundaries and how much we can put up with each other.'

Grooming at Badminton is always highly regarded among the many grooms on the eventing circuit and when Ian asked Ruth if she would look after Glenburnie in 1990 she jumped at the chance. Ian was also taking Murphy who was under the charge of Douglas Edward who was working for Ian at the time. While Ian was away competing in France just before Badminton there was a sudden panic when Glen injured himself and was suddenly left with a swollen leg. Not being able to get in touch with Ian and after much discussion with everyone on the yard it was decided they would give him a shot of penicillin, forgetting it was a banned substance. On realising what they had done the quiet panic of earlier turned into full-blown pandemonium with no one daring to tell Ian what they had done.

Ruth remembers: 'It was a very worrying time and we were in constant touch with the vet who took blood samples. On the morning we set off for Badminton the vet spent ages chasing Glen round his stable to try and get a urine sample. When we arrived at the stables at Badminton we weren't allowed in until the test came back negative which was a huge relief and it was all systems go again.'

With the temperature well into the 70s it was a scorching week and Ruth and Douglas had an agreement. Ruth would feed the horses first thing in the morning as he was so bad at getting up, but once she called for him he had to climb out of his bed. Glenburnie was second to go and Ruth was well aware that if Ian was late the whole event would be held up. After an unlucky stop coming out of the water when he stumbled up the bank to the upturned boat Glenburnie finished the event in 15th place. Murphy collected 17.6 time penalties on the cross-country, giving Ian a difficult ride pulling all the way to claim 14th place.

Ruth felt grooming Glenburnie at Badminton was quite an initiation as it was the first time she had groomed at a three-day event. For a few years she always took the horses back to Stowell Park, about 40 minutes away, after Badminton to relieve Ian and Jenny of that responsibility. When the horses were loaded in 1990 she thought it would be appropriate to thank the Duke of Beaufort for his hospitality during the event and laughs when remembering the expression on his face. 'I don't think a groom had ever thanked him before and then I nearly ran him over with the lorry but the set-up and organisation at Badminton is so good for the grooms I just felt it would be nice to say thank you.'

In between her first Badminton and grooming for Arakai in 1997, Ruth looked after Stanwick Ghost at Blenheim and missed out at a number of the major events as horses sustained injuries and didn't go to the event. Ruth was all set to go to Badminton in 1996 with Lord and Lady Vestey's Mr Mackinnon but he injured a leg and was withdrawn.

Lord and Lady Vestey bought Clan Royal for Ian to ride and he remains Ruth's favourite horse although she also had a soft spot for Griffin and Charlie Brown. 'All Ian's horses over the years have had something likeable about them but Clan Royal just stands out for me and he was always my favourite. I love chestnut horses so that probably helped and as he always managed to have a leg injury of some kind I seemed to spend a lot of time with him trying to get him sound again. He first damaged a tendon at Thirlestane and then a year later damaged the other leg. His first injury showed up after his dressage and cross-country. We pulled him out of the lorry for the show-jumping only to find he was lame and when I started to walk him in the hope it would wear off he just got worse and worse and had to be box rested for weeks.'

Ruth groomed Clan Royal at Punchestown for Ian and remembers having a very enjoyable time in Ireland despite not being able to watch the show-jumping and feeling quite deflated when he had the first fence down. Preferring to watch the rain come across towards the event Ruth sat quietly listening to the groan from the crowd but was still delighted when her favourite chestnut finished eighth.

Ruth says the first few years helping Ian were very enjoyable and it is only in recent years with Mr Mackinnon, who was quite temperamental, that she

Ruth Day with Mr Mackinnon (Tim Smith)

felt more pressure. The arrival of Arakai intensified this feeling and when he was staying at Stowell Park in the few days before the Open European Championships in 1997 she had a number of sleepless nights. 'When Lord and Lady Vestey bought Mr Mackinnon I liked him instantly but he was so quick and sharp that you could never really relax with him or trust him with people who don't know one hundred per cent what they are doing. There have been many times when he has been impossible to catch in the field and he drives you quite mad.'

One of the most tear-jerking times for Ruth came at Burghley in 1995 when a relatively young Mr Mackinnon came galloping through the cross-country finish and went on to complete in ninth place. Ian was second to go and when Eddie Stibbe pulled up quite early no one knew how the course would ride. Ruth was helping Caroline Powell, Ian's head girl at the time, and admits there wasn't a dry eye in the house. The horse had jumped round Burghley for fun and although he was tiring towards the end he kept on jumping and trying.

When Ruth was leading Mr Mackinnon up to the show-jumping on the final day they met the hound box and he threw himself around in blind panic, pulling away from Ruth and heading off towards the car park. Luckily another rider managed to catch him and they made their way steadily to the main arena with the other horse as a lead. With just one fence down they finished in the top ten and everyone thought Ian had another star in the making. But as so often happens disappointment was to follow. He was resting at Stowell Park and he had been brought in from the field for the day as they were hunting in the area. Ruth found some heat in one of his legs and it was assumed he had somehow knocked himself. The vet was called and started to treat him, and a horse walker was quickly installed in the hope it would aid his treatment. He gradually improved and travelled up to Haughhead just after Christmas in preparation for the new season. A respiratory problem had been cleared up and all was going well but Ian felt he wasn't quite right and was concerned his leg might not stand the rigours of Badminton and he was withdrawn at the last minute to be given a year off.

Returning to Stowell Park, Mr Mackinnon finally went back to Ian's in the spring of 1997 where he continued to live out most of the time to help both his breathing and his temperament which remained as explosive as during his formative years. With Mr Mackinnon off the road Lord and Lady Vestey decided to buy another horse for Ian and chose the hugely talented Arakai who had arrived in the country during the winter of 1996 with Vaughn Jefferis.

Says Ruth: 'The first time I saw Arakai was when I was sent along to supervise his vetting. Lady Vestey was very interested in another New Zealand horse but Ian had suggested they go and have a look at Arakai because he was already in this country with Vaughn. Everyone thought he was very talented and Ian decided to take him to Boekelo in Holland towards the end of the season. I flew out with Lady Vestey for the cross-country and show-jumping and it was very exciting to be involved with such a top-class horse again. He had a glance-off on the cross-country but showed how much scope he had and I thought his show-jumping round was one of the best I had ever seen Ian jump.

'Arakai is so talented and that can often make everything so much more intense. During the winter while he was at Stowell Park resting he managed to strike into himself and the deep bruising was always worrying. Fortunately his spring events in the run up to Badminton went very well and despite his obvious potential we tried to treat him as normally as we could.'

Ruth describes Badminton 1997 as especially nerve-wracking with Arakai. Every time she opened a magazine the press were writing such great things about Lord and Lady Vestey's new horse that it put a lot of pressure on the team and everyone was very aware how easily accidents can happen. Ian's two Badminton rides were in capable hands for 1997, Ruth looking after Arakai and Sharon Kitson who works for Lady Hartington caring for Stanwick Ghost. They left Stowell Park in high spirits and made the short journey to Badminton and were pleased they had been given stables at one end, out of the way and in a quiet area that would suit the horses. Says Ruth: 'Every time Ian took Stanwick Ghost out to give him some work Arakai tried to climb the walls and we couldn't leave him. Everyone was pleased with Arakai's test, which came on a blustery morning, and despite moments when he became very tense it was good to see him relax again. It was an early start for the cross-country and everything seemed a total blur.'

'One minute I was trying to watch the television monitors and the next minute he was galloping through the finish. There was one slight panic when Ian lost his inhaler after the steeplechase but luckily we found it. Because they were on so early we saw more of the round than we probably would have and once they finished there was an incredible atmosphere, everyone was hugging each other as the round meant so much to everyone and it was such a relief they had got home safely.

'Somewhere on the course Arakai had managed to graze his stifle. We think he caught himself at the Quarry by which time he was probably getting a little tired and once all the excitement had calmed down and I'd led him out for some grass to try and settle him I started icing his leg.' The icing and physiotherapy continued well into the night in the hope of easing the stiffness and when Ian rode him out the following morning the hard work proved worthwhile. Despite signs of slight stiffness he was sound and passed the trot-up without any worries.

Ruth describes the show-jumping as stomach churning and when the heavens opened she made her way, slipping and slithering, to the main arena with Arakai. 'Ian didn't over jump Arakai and I just kept my eyes closed; there was no way I could watch. He hit just one fence and Ian blamed himself for the error. There was a long wait then until Stanwick Ghost went and, wanting to keep them apart, I took Arakai off to try and shelter under the trees and spent the rest of the afternoon keeping him on the move.

'I must have walked miles round the trees and I think everyone thought I was quite mad, then suddenly it went silent as Ian went in on Stanwick Ghost. I didn't know what was happening or how many fences he had down and it was actually quite a relief to be on my own. It was all very disappointing and no one really knew what to say and I really felt for Ian and Lady Hartington.

'Both horses were asked to stay another night so they could be presented early the following morning for the selectors and then we brought everything back to Stowell Park. Arakai was turned out for a rest with Lord Vestey's old hunter Gambir and Stanwick Ghost went off to Newmarket for a check-up. Ian had been concerned about his breathing after he was quite slow to recover from the cross-country but tests showed there was nothing to be worried about and everyone was shocked when leg problems were revealed which saw him having the rest of the season off.'

Having groomed at Badminton, Ruth took a back seat role throughout the Open Europeans at Burghley leaving the task to Vicky Welton, with Ruth helping out when needed. Says Ruth: 'We were all very excited about the Europeans as it was the first time Lady Vestey had a horse competing in a major championships but this also put a lot of pressure on everyone at Stowell Park who follow Ian's efforts so closely.'

Sharon Kitson and Jenny wait for Ian to finish Phase A, Badminton 1997 (Tim Smith)

• • •

Sharon Kitson has worked as head groom for Lady Hartington for ten years. She first groomed for Ian at Glenluce in 1994. Says Sharon: 'I was asked by Lady Hartington if I would like to groom for Ian and Stanwick Ghost at Badminton. I accepted the offer but felt rather sick with nerves at what I was taking on as it was over 12 years since I had been on the eventing circuit but I like a challenge and this was what I was going to get.

'It was arranged that I would go and help Ian at Glenluce, as I felt I was rather rusty with the eventing routine. Ian had a slight problem for this event in that he had no transport so Lady Hartington agreed to lend him her horsebox which was a lot smaller than he was used to and I was amazed how much Ian could get in the lorry including four horses. To say that it was packed to the roof is not an overstatement! I remember the journey being rather a "white knuckle" ride, and I was amazed at the speeds Ian could reach in our little wagon, on the narrow, twisty roads in Scotland, but Ian was totally relaxed and unworried.

'Getting down to the stables when we arrived at the event was a real work of art, as it was extremely wet, but Ian seemed to have the ability to get a horsebox where it really does not want to go, and after a few rather spectacular "half passes" the wagon was parked up for the weekend, right next to the stables. With the horses out of the lorry and settled in I then learnt a very good lesson on how to plait in the dark. We managed to get four horses done, but I dreaded to think what they would look like in daylight.

'That evening we seemed to accumulate more and more people and ended up with seven people sleeping in a wagon with no sleeping accommodation. Everyone seemed to crash out at midnight, but were kept awake by a horse kicking its box most of the night. Ian was heard to go out and hurl abuse at some horse, and came back muttering that he didn't know if it was the right one, but it made him feel better. The event went well and Jack won his section. He was now bound for Badminton.

'Badminton was a very different experience to the relaxed atmosphere of Glenluce. It was very enjoyable, but hard work with a lot of pressure. I found it particularly difficult not really knowing Ian and his routine for a three-day, but I was basically left to look after Jack, and didn't really see that much of Ian, who said it was quite strange just having one horse to concentrate on.

'Jenny was a great support, and was always there to help when needed. She is truly remarkable, remaining calm in any situation and I can imagine that Ian tests her to the extreme at times! Thankfully things seemed to run fairly smoothly, until the dreadful cross-country when Jack tipped up at the Quarry and was cast against the wall. With great sadness Ian retired, and my first Badminton came to an abrupt end. Jack was loaded on to the lorry, everything was packed up and we headed back to Stowell Park with a huge air of disappointment surrounding us.

'It was several months before I saw Ian and Jenny again but I saw a lot of Jack as he came to stay at Lady Hartington's after he sustained an injury later in the season and I was responsible for him while he was recuperating. Jack has to be my favourite of all Ian's horses. He always has such presence about him, but can be rather grumpy when he is on strict rations. All Ian's horses seem to have a devilish streak in them, and more often than not, love to give the grooms a hard time.

'I had the thrilling job of exercising Jack after a long period of box rest and while walking in hand was not easy, exercising was something else. I remember the first few days' exercising very well. Lady Hartington accompanied me on her lovely and very sensitive hunter mare, but it wasn't to make a great deal of difference. Jack was rather high-spirited but all was well and nothing much happened until a gentleman drove past and stopped, got out of his car to ask directions and got back into his car and shut the door. This was just the excuse Jack needed, and it was his cue to explode. He leapt so high off the floor that I thought we were never coming back down! Lady Hartington was very amused. Thankfully we returned back to Beamsley in one piece, and his exercising was rather less eventful after that. Jack made a good recovery and went back up to Ian's, and we really missed him.

'The last time I groomed for Ian was Badminton 1997. I felt a lot happier having been there previously, and had a good idea what to expect. It was also very pleasant having Ruth Day grooming for Arakai. She has a wonderful sense of humour, which seems to make all the difference when situations are getting tense. It is really difficult to describe the emotions that I felt at Badminton that year, from being so high after the dressage and the cross-country to such a low after the show-jumping.

'I remember walking Jack round in the pouring rain, waiting to go into the ring. Initially it was full of horses, but as time went on they grew less and less, until eventually there were just Jack and me walking round and how lonely it felt.

'When I got him back to the stables after the disastrous show-jumping, it was almost as if he knew. He was so miserable and just stood at the back of his box, and I found it very sad how nobody really wanted to know him afterwards apart from Lady Hartington who came to see him, and had a talk to him. It just seemed so strange from having people all week wanting to see him, and making all the fuss of Arakai next door, who had done brilliantly for such a young horse. I suppose it was being so closely involved with such a special horse that I felt so sad for him.' It was to be even more depressing news later that week when it was discovered he had sustained a tendon injury.

New Zealander Caroline Powell, née Turner, was based with Ian for two years. Her stint at Haughhead including grooming for Stanwick Ghost at the Atlanta Olympics. Caroline had worked in a number of yards before moving to the Starks and in fact rode Caliber for Clive and Jane Storey at Bramham to finish 12th before Ian was given the ride.

'After working for Polly Lochore breaking and producing horses during the winter I rang Ian and Jenny to see if there were any vacancies,' says Caroline. 'At the time they had about 18 horses around and were very busy so I was quickly thrown into the role. In the stables there was Stanwick Ghost, Mr Mackinnon, Clan Royal, Forest Glen and Sir Marcus as well as lots of youngsters so we had plenty to do.

'I remember Mr Mackinnon being very hard work and neurotic but once he started to trust you he changed and became quite friendly towards you. Stanwick Ghost was a great character and always had tricks up his sleeve. During my first year with Ian we went practically everywhere and I thoroughly enjoyed being on the road gaining experience. When we went out to Saumur it was my first three-day event and turned out to be a very entertaining trip. Everyone was given meal tickets that we managed to swap for wine and before we knew it the loo was fit to burst with bottles. When I looked after Caliber at Badminton the atmosphere was so different to just about all the other three-day events. Usually there is quite a big focus on socialising but at Badminton everyone is very serious and there is so much at stake.

'The first time Forest Glen went to Bramham in 1995 he had a run out when I was grooming and then when he won the following year I was at home and an Australian working pupil went to the event. Grooming for Jack in Atlanta was quite an experience but I don't think anyone can prepare you for what you are going to face at an Olympics.

'As if going to the Olympics wasn't enough I got married two days before I went. We had been up at Burgie and once we finished there I drove back to Kelso and then down to Birmingham to pick up my Olympic kit. Ian had gone to London to get his and the following day it was my wedding. Everything was such a rush with last minute packing but luckily working in such a well established yard as Ian's we had everything we needed for Atlanta. Before heading for the Olympics we travelled south to Badminton for five days of team training and took along Moose who had just arrived. Everything went smoothly and I was chosen as one of the three grooms to travel out with the horses to Atlanta.

'Grooming for Jack and Leslie Law's ride New Flavour during the flight gave me plenty to do and while the horses were in quarantine we had a few days to relax after the long journey. It was about four days before Ian got to see Jack and I was relieved that everything had gone so smoothly at this stage. The horses were transported to an equestrian base called Pine Tops where we had about three weeks to acclimatise in preparation for the event.

'When we were transferred to the Olympic venue we realised no amount of money had been spared for the horses – the set up was just amazing. Everything had been meticulously planned to the last detail and there was a wonderful veterinary clinic in case of emergencies. The waiting was quite a stressful time but I was pleased with how Jack was coping with the intense heat and thought that being grey probably helped.

'Once the event started it was a complete whirl of activity and after his fabulous dressage Jack thought he was such a star and posed with incredible ease. His test put everyone in a good mood but as Ian was based off the complex with the other riders I felt a lot of responsibility in making sure Jack was well for the cross-country. The cross-country started very early in the morning and the heat that everyone had been so concerned about never really materialised which was a great relief. Jack set off looking a picture while everyone stood watching the television cameras nervously. When he fell at the water it was quite devastating. Everyone had put in so much work and effort to get to the Olympics and it was so uncharacteristic for either Ian or Jack to make a mistake on the cross-country. As soon as they got home I spent every spare minute hosing and icing Jack's legs and chest. He had a swelling on his chest and I kept on working right up until the trot-up the next day.

'When he passed it made all the work seem worth it. Although everyone felt quite down about the team's performance there was still the individual event to come and everyone supported each other. Ian travelled home and I remember that once the individual event was over it was actually quite a relief to get on the plane despite the amazing experience only an Olympics can provide.

'Having swapped roles with the other grooms who flew home with the horses, I finally met up with Jack again 14 hours later and was pleased to load him on to the lorry and head for Yorkshire to Lady Hartington's where he was left for a well earned rest. The Olympics had been a great experience but quite stressful in a way and when I returned to Haughhead, I realised it was time to move on. I was very tired and felt I couldn't give Ian the full commitment he needed. I had learnt so much during my stay and the six weeks away in Atlanta were wonderful, even though I did get teased about going away on honeymoon with Jack instead of Richard my husband. I knew it was time to try to put into practice the knowledge I had gained. As a groom you get very little time to yourself and are part of a team that requires everyone to pull their weight and the Olympics was a great way to end two years at Haughhead.'

. . .

Vicky Welton started grooming for Ian full-time after spending two summers at Haughhead getting to know the set-up and learning Ian's philosophy on training and competing top-class event horses. The highlight of the 1997 season at Haughhead was grooming at the Open Europeans for Arakai while Moose's fifth place at Blenheim also comes high on her list of events to remember. Moose is her favourite horse and Vicky was over the moon when he did so well and says she always had every faith in him.

'I first met Ian at a lecture demonstration he was holding at my parents' base, Tower Farm saddlers near Rugby,' says Vicky. 'He had brought a team of horses and I thought the whole display was fascinating. My mother asked Ian if I could go to Haughhead for a few weeks in the summer and it went from there. The following summer I returned and then in 1997 I became head girl. I have ridden for most of my life and used to belong to the North Warwickshire Pony Club so I had quite a good start for working with horses full-time.

'We spend endless hours on the road but it is all part of the job and something you get used to. The events abroad are always a wonderful experience and I will always remember Boekelo in 1996 for the large amount of free lager there was for everyone as Grolsch sponsored the event. Punchestown is also a fun event as is Blair Castle where there is always a great atmosphere. Floors Castle was quite remarkable. Positive Rain had arrived the night before after Jonquil Hemming asked Ian if he would ride the horse at Bramham. He sat on him for the first time at the event and was given a 19 for his dressage. The test was amazing and just showed what a rider Ian is – not many would have been able to get such a good result out of the horse in such a short space of time.

'I spent Badminton 1997 commuting from Stowell Park while Ruth Day and Sharon Kitson looked after Arakai and Stanwick Ghost. When Stanwick Ghost hit five fences I think it was probably the worst moment of my life. Once Badminton was over Ian was competing at Punchestown so Stephanie and I kept the horses exercised ready for that event. Working for Ian and Jenny you are part of the family and being quite a small team now it is important that everyone gets on well.

'Of all the horses in the yard I have an especially soft spot for Moose. He thinks he is so big and tough but is really just a friendly giant. He sticks his head in the air when you are trying to put his bridle on but once its on he knows who the boss is. Stanwick Ghost can be very funny to ride out and starts to have a tantrum if he is out for more than 45 minutes, stamping his feet on the ground like a spoilt child, but Arakai is lovely to hack out and very talented.

'On the whole Ian is good to work for and is quite relaxed. If he is on form he has a great sense of humour but when things go wrong it is better to be out of the way – like anyone he is only human and tempers can flare on the odd occasion. At Boekelo I had ten minutes to get Arakai ready for his dressage and that was quite a tense time and I just thought why couldn't someone else be there. Ian is very particular about his own and the horses' appearance and does expect high standards.

'Jenny is the one who pulls everything together and is very organised. We think of her as "the organisation" and it is a good job she knows what everyone should be doing at any time. Both Ian and Jenny are still very enthusiastic about eventing and everyone says the set-up will carry on as long as there is that enthusiasm. If that goes I think Ian will just stop rather than gradually slow down. Jenny and Ian get on so well and Ian admits he relies on her. Now and again you find him in the kitchen doing a spot of cooking but the one thing he doesn't do very often is muck out. If we are pushed for time Ian always helps out plaiting and prefers to pull manes and tails himself then if they are not right he only has himself to blame.

Vicky Welton at Bramham with Positive Rain

'At many of the events the owners come along to watch and are very good at helping when we need another pair of hands and Lady Hartington always brings excellent picnics to feed everyone. She is very involved with her horses and is very enthusiastic for the team.

'Being based in Scotland the other grooms on the circuit think it must be quiet but during the season we are on the road so much that we are never at Haughhead for long. When we are there we appreciate the peace and quiet. Anyone working for Ian is expected to use their common sense and there is the opportunity to learn so much in a top eventing yard. Ian does care about his horses and even if there are problems he never gets off and flings the reins at me.

'Even Tim who doesn't ride plays a part mending the fences and keeping the place tidy. Being a similar age to Stephanie we get on very well and are good friends. Ian and Jenny are very supportive of her riding but understand she doesn't want to event professionally and only push her so far. Ian gets very nervous for Stephanie and I'm sure would rather be riding himself. When she was on the British junior team at Blair it was very exciting. A lot of us felt people probably thought she was only on the team because she was Ian's daughter but she had a very good season and deserved to be on the team. She is very like Ian and definitely has a temper!

'A typical day in the yard is to have the horses fed by 7.30 a.m. before they are skipped out and then the riding starts straight after breakfast, followed by tack cleaning, yard duties and the evening feed. Those riding try to get the second lot out by 11 a.m. while one of the team stays behind to help Ian with any horse he wants to jump after schooling. Lunch wouldn't be the same without a break to watch *Neighbours* – a Stark ritual. Ian isn't the best person in the world at getting up unless we are off to an event and can't go anywhere without his supply of Coca-Cola and chocolate.

'During the season we are so busy that no one takes much time off and then when the last event comes round and everything stops the feeling is very odd. The adrenaline that has kept you going from spring to autumn suddenly disappears and you can start to slow down and actually think about how the events have gone. Haughhead is always full of people and the diary so busy with work and social engagements that when the season ends everyone is ready for some breathing space.'

9

Owners, Supporters, Friends and Sponsors

'Ian used to be terrified of me and Barbara Slane Fleming. One day at Floors Castle Horse Trials we both approached Ian from opposite sides and I think he hoped the ground would swallow him up.'

FRIEND, SUPPORTER AND HORSE GRAZER PHOEBE STEWART

Ian is the first to recognise that without the many owners and supporters it would have been impossible to achieve the success that has come his way. To Ian and especially Jenny, Dame Jean Maxwell-Scott will always be a special owner because she was one of the first people they became heavily involved with and because she was the joint owner of Sir Wattie, everyone's favourite.

When Ian decided his days as a civil servant were numbered and his desire to work with horses full-time became more realistic, Jenny spent many anxious moments wondering how they were going to pay the bills and keep a roof over their heads. And when in the summer of 1984, after Ian had been so successful at Badminton with Oxford Blue and Sir Wattie, The Edinburgh Woollen Mill stepped in to sponsor four horses, everyone started to look a little further into the future.

'When The Edinburgh Woollen Mill helped us, in the form of David and Alix Stevenson I was incredibly relieved,' admits Jenny. 'We had been chatting to our accountant who also did work for The Edinburgh Woollen Mill and the cash flow was starting to become a serious problem. Luckily everything gelled at the right time and we were incredibly lucky it all took off when it did. Their financial help took the pressure off, leaving Ian to concentrate on competing, knowing that we could afford to run the lorry. Many people couldn't understand why we didn't move south but I wanted to be based in the Borders, with two small children it was difficult on the eventing scene which at the best of times is not really a family sport.

'When The Edinburgh Woollen Mill decided to change direction with their sponsorship we were fortunate again when Lord and Lady Vestey offered to buy Ian a horse and then Lord and Lady Hartington also offered their support surrounded by the many firms that help us with products and equipment.'

Dame Jean Maxwell-Scott was one of Ian's earliest owners, joint owning Sir Wattie with her great friend Susan Luczyc-Wyhowska until The Edinburgh Woollen Mill bought Susan's share. Says Dame Jean: 'I must have seen Ian when he was quite young following the hunt and I often saw Jenny and her parents out hunting with the Duke of Buccleuch. Jenny's mother, Jean McAulay, has always been a friend and when we sent Wattie to Ian our connections grew stronger. Wattie came about as Susan and I had always admired a strawberry roan mare called Rosie that belonged to Major Hugh Cairns. When the day came to retire the mare from the hunting field she was sent to the good stallion Bronze Hill with Wattie the result.

'Wattie was born at Wooden near Kelso but when he was six weeks old he was moved to Abbotsford as the grass at Wooden had become too rich for him. I then saw plenty of him during his formative years, his time divided between the two places. Bill Hughes, a friend who lives nearby, started to work on Wattie and saw a great deal of potential in him. Wattie had developed into a striking bay with plenty of character and once he was old enough Bill suggested Wattie be sent to Ian for schooling.' When Wattie developed an angleberry a Mr Armitage who was well known in the area sorted out the problem with one of his special mixtures and came back some time later when Wattie developed a problem with his back, which he soon put right.

Wattie derived his name from Sir Walter Scott, the romantic poet and novelist who lived at Abbotsford. Dame Jean is Sir Walter Scott's great, great, great-granddaughter and Wattie was also born on her father's birthday, which helped to make him extra special. A horse from the Borders, owned by two people from the Borders and ridden by a rider from the Borders it was no wonder he had such a following in the area.

The partnership started in 1980 and was to see Ian and Wattie take the honours at two Badmintons as well as collect numerous championship medals throughout their reign. Dame Jean's early recollections of Ian's time with

Wattie include his first attempt at riding him in an indoor school when the young and inexperienced horse tried to put Ian through the roof. In a bid to offer Ian some financial support to help with the cost of competing, Dame Jean sold his full brother and started to follow Ian's career closely travelling out to the Los Angeles and Seoul Olympics to watch him in action. She remembers their first big win coming early on at Fenton Horse Trials in Northumberland when they came home with two silver trophies much to everyone's surprise.

Wattie's counterpart Oxford Blue was chosen for the Los Angeles Olympics in preference to Wattie but Dame Jean remembers clearly the intense heat of the event and helped out with feedback on the cross-country course at the Fairbanks ranch. She has many happy memories of her trips to Badminton, when Wattie was sixth in 1984 at his first attempt, and then twice a winner. She describes the wins as incredibly exciting and quite thrilling but she always found it very difficult to watch the show-jumping and rarely bothered to waste money on grandstand seats. 'I could never bare to watch,' she laughs. 'At one of the Badmintons I was near the front of the stand when a lady saw the owner's badge I was wearing and said, "Oh that is the one we want to win", referring to Wattie. Whether it was his name that caught everyone's attention I don't know. In the early days the school children were always shown round the stables and they always wanted to see Wattie.'

One of the highlights of her association with Ian was the trip out to Seoul for the Olympics in 1988. A long journey for everyone concerned, the horses flew to Moscow for refuelling before continuing the journey while Jenny and Dame Jean travelled out together on an organised tour.

'Travelling around to watch Ian and Wattie I gradually got to know quite a lot of people in the eventing world and everyone was very friendly. I had no idea Korea was going to be so pretty and there was this huge modern city I just hadn't expected with the people having a real love of flowers. The fences on the cross-country course were wonderful and one of the jumps was supposed to be a colourful vegetable cart but the fruit had gone off and the smell was terrible. Our accommodation was in the red light district which caused a great deal of amusement. The night after Ian had won two silver medals we went out for a meal to celebrate and I was given a card so that we would get back to the hotel. Everyone looked at the card and had a laugh at the address but the hotel was actually very clean. During the Olympics I think everyone in the Borders stayed up late to watch the television and everyone was very excited. It was an amazing time and I feel very fortunate to have been part of that. Ian, Jenny, Stephanie and Tim are a remarkable family and very hardworking while Ian has always appeared totally fearless. He is very dedicated and never gives up trying.'

Following the success at Seoul Dame Jean hosted a party at Abbotsford. Everyone remotely connected to Wattie from the farrier to the vet was invited to the lunch party with Wattie also there to enjoy the occasion. During Wattie's rest periods he always returned to Abbotsford to be with his old friend, Bunny the white donkey. 'It was wonderful to have a horse like Wattie and be involved with Ian and Jenny. For most people it remains a dream to own a top-class horse and I count myself very lucky to have had so much fun. I shall always remember the trip to Seoul and how supportive The Edinburgh Woollen Mill were throughout their involvement as joint owners of Wattie.'

During 1997 after a lengthy spell without a horse at Haughhead, Dame Jean sent another homebred horse, the talented Douce Davie for Stephanie to ride and enjoyed again the ups and downs of having a horse with the Starks.

• • •

David and Alix Stevenson could not have stepped into Ian and Jenny's life at a more appropriate time than in 1984 when they offered to sponsor the team under The Edinburgh Woollen Mill banner. The deal included support for the horses, team clothing, a new lorry and more importantly the financial security, which put Ian's bank manager at ease.

With a wonderfully successful business, David Stevenson decided that not only would his company benefit from sponsoring Ian, by raising its profile and gaining national coverage but it was also a way of putting something back into the local community. Ian had just finished third and sixth at his first Badminton and with a big following in the area a connection with The Edinburgh Woollen Mill would benefit everyone. And so it was that between 1984 and 1992 the company based just a few miles down the road from Ian at Langholm supported the team.

It was a partnership that carried Ian and The Edinburgh Woollen Mill's name to the Los Angeles Olympics, followed by Seoul and finally Barcelona. David Stevenson, a former Olympic pole vaulter, was delighted to know that the business he had helped to make so successful could help Ian stay at the top. Throughout their association he enjoyed an excellent relationship with all the team, going along to support at many events and major occasions while at the same time allowing Ian the space he needed to concentrate fully on riding and competing. The support certainly helped Ian to stay at the top and he is very grateful for the help and assistance The Edinburgh Woollen Mill provided. Ian was under a lot of pressure to move south with all the travelling involved, but Jenny didn't want to and with a Scottish sponsor on board that need to move slipped away.

David and Alix Stevenson at Burghley with Glenburnie (left) *and Murphy Himself. With Jenny is Mark Holliday who tragically was killed in a fall at Hexham a few years later*

'I first met Ian in the 1970s,' says David. 'I used to ride for a hobby, going hunting and taking part in the common ridings and a few competitions in which Ian always came first and I finished last. Ian and I both used the same accountant and when Ian was set to go to Los Angeles he suggested I might look at sponsoring Ian. As a former athlete I had always said if the money was available I would try to put something back into sport and decided to get involved. Ian wasn't in a position like some of the riders in the south who were from wealthy backgrounds and the cost of travelling from the north could have prevented him from competing around the country. The sponsorship worked well for The Edinburgh Woollen Mill, helping to raise our profile with people who were interested in buying our clothing and visiting the shops which are mostly in the country and market towns. Over the years the business became synonymous with Ian and the agreement worked very well.

'Out of all the horses in the yard throughout our involvement I always really liked Glenburnie and Sir Wattie who were great characters. Travelling out to both Seoul and Barcelona I remember there was a great deal of camaraderie and it was quite like being in your own little world. The Olympics were fascinating occasions and we have some very happy memories of the trips.'

David feels Ian's success over the years has been helped by the natural empathy he has with the horses he rides and his love of danger, while being able to accommodate the pressure at major events has played its part. He also acknowledges the key role played by Jenny, encouraging Ian to put more effort into the dressage and flatwork side of the business.

. . .

Phoebe Stewart came into Ian's life relatively early in his career. For 18 years she lived just four miles away at Midlem where she farmed 280 acres with her husband Duggie Stewart, the Olympic medallist who won a show-jumping gold medal at Helsinki in 1952. Land on the farm was set aside to graze the resting horses or those that Ian felt needed a change of scene from the busy activity at Haughhead.

A keen hunt follower, Phoebe was always more than happy to take any of Ian's horses needing a change of scene and she watched his eventing career closely often turning out at events to support him. She is also close to Stephanie and on many occasions·took her back to school near Edinburgh when Jenny was busy.

Says Phoebe: 'We used to have eight horses at a time on occasions. Ian felt when they were away from home they switched off and it always seemed that they appeared in the hours of darkness. Having the land to graze the horses I was useful to Ian and enjoyed having the horses come to stay. When Murphy first came to the farm he didn't particularly like people and was quite wary of them. I used to carry a stick for the sheep but when I went into the field with him I would put it down otherwise he would be very cautious about coming up to me. I simply adored Murphy; he was an incredible character. When Ian first brought him to Midlem he rode him down the drive bare back with just a head collar and lead rope.

'For eight-and-a-half years I was the *chef d'equipe* for the British paralympic team and the last person to ride Murphy was Jo Jackson who won three gold medals in Atlanta with the team. Jo wanted to experience the feel of riding a top-class horse and Murphy gave her that chance. A week later he was at Midlem when we found him with a broken hock with no sign of how he had injured himself and it was a very sad day.

'All the horses I bred went to Ian and for a while Stephanie also rode a horse called Smarty for me. I had a half share in Stephanie's young horse Higgins, who was Murphy's nephew, but sadly he had to be put down before he started competing. I sent four of my young horses to Ian because I knew they would be properly produced and given the chance of being successful.

'When Jack first arrived at the farm he was quite naughty but to me never stood out in the same way as Murphy. I had to laugh when Ian brought Mix N' Match along. He was a big piebald horse and Ian didn't realise I couldn't bear coloured horses.

'Ian is just a natural and I think it was quite a struggle in the early days and a big relief when The Edinburgh Woollen Mill stepped in with sponsorship. Without that backing I think it would have been quite impossible with all the expense involved. The whole family are wonderful people and very helpful and willing to assist others. Ian is the vice-president of the Border region of the Riding for the Disabled Association and will always present prizes or turn up to events when asked if he is in the country. I used to take Stephanie back to school and this gave us the opportunity to talk about horses and whether she would like to follow in Ian's footsteps. She is very bright and hardworking but I think she will choose to pursue a career away from horses, preferring to compete without the added pressure of earning a living from them. Tim is so very different and will always be successful as he can turn his hand to anything and is very practical so I don't think Ian and Jenny have too much to worry about.'

• • •

Lord and Lady Vestey's offer to use Stowell Park as a southern base could not have come at a better time than it did in the early months of 1987. Ian and Jenny were trying to plan the programme for the year, wondering how they could keep up the non-stop travelling and when the offer arrived there was no way they were going to turn it down. Set in motion by Lady Vestey's sister Henrietta Knight, who was then chairman of the selectors, the spring move to Stowell Park has continued ever since and makes the start of the season so much easier for Ian and Jenny.

They visited the estate on a Friday in late February and by the Monday had moved in much to everyone's surprise at the speed of their arrival. The first week was a complete daze as they tried to get everyone settled and Ian sat his BHSI Stable Manager's exam at Stoneleigh on the Friday. Sandra Miller and Cassy Carruthers were helping with the horses at the time and while Jenny kept up the horses' fittening work those two tried to make the set-up as organised as possible. Working towards Badminton in the spring with Wattie everything was going well until torrential rain led to the event being cancelled and it was left to Lady Vestey to tell Ian the bad news after all the effort that had gone into the preparations.

Lady Vestey recalls: 'I first met Ian and Jenny when they came to look round Stowell Park. My sister had said the Starks were looking for a base in the south and would we consider Stowell Park. We had plenty of stables, which had housed the polo ponies before we started to cut back and we felt there was enough space to accommodate everyone while allowing life at Stowell Park to continue as normal.

'When they came to look round I think they saw the place would be suitable and were quite amazed by the room but I was quite taken aback when I asked them when they intended to move down and the reply was in a couple of days. Their arrival with countless horses, two children, dogs and grooms was quite memorable but soon everything was sorted and life carried on as before but probably at a slightly quicker pace. At first they lived in a cottage near to the bottom stable yard and Stephanie and Tim went to school at Chedworth a couple of miles away. We decided they would have free run with the horses at the top yard so they could completely take them over and have their own routine while we could carry on as before.'

By then Ian had retired Oxford Blue his ride at the Los Angeles Olympics and 11th at the World Championships in Australia in 1986. He hunted for the following two seasons and then ran in two hunter chases before it was suggested he would make a good hunter for Lady Vestey who regularly hunted with the Beaufort. Robbie proved a bold, strong hunter and he gave his new rider some wonderful days.

On one occasion Lady Vestey asked her head girl Ruth Day if she could take a photograph of Robbie jumping a stone wall. But when the photograph was developed and revealed how unbecoming Robbie looked with his tail stuck in the air, plaited and tied up to stop it trailing in the mud she said never again would a horse she was riding have its tail tied in such a fashion. Their partnership also led to them competing in the first Comic Relief flat race at Cheltenham which was a momentous occasion and put to the test Lady Vestey's many earlier rides in flat races. Eventually after a number of happy years together Robbie injured his hock and Lady Vestey and Ian decided to have him put down quietly as he would no longer be able to lead the active life he so enjoyed.

'Robbie was a wonderful horse but Glenburnie was my favourite as I love thoroughbreds and he was bred to be a racehorse,' says Lady Vestey. 'He was bred to win the Gold Cup and as a child I rode out chasers and will always choose a thoroughbred in preference for any other horse and that is why I like Arakai so much. Clan Royal was the first horse we bought for Ian from The Edinburgh Woollen Mill and Mr Mackinnon followed. We could have bought Stanwick Ghost but as we had just taken on Mr Mackinnon, I asked my great friend Amanda Hartington if she was interested in owning a horse for Ian to ride and everyone always reminds us we could have had the grey.

'When Mr Mackinnon was laid off with his legs we decided to look for another horse and bought Arakai. I had said to my husband that I'd always wanted a New Zealand thoroughbred and when Ian found Harry we were very

Owners Lady Vestey (left) *and Lady Hartington at Badminton 1997* (Tim Smith)

excited. When Ian and everyone comes to stay at Stowell Park the place is much more hectic and everyone on the estate adores them. Over the years everyone on the farm and estate has followed Ian's career closely and we are all very proud when he does well. The whole team is such a part of Stowell Park and everyone is very supportive.'

• • •

Lady Hartington is the proud owner of four of Ian's rides, Jack, better known as Stanwick Ghost, The Moose and the newest acquisitions Jaybee, another New Zealand thoroughbred and Saucy Brown. She now spends a great deal of her time supporting the team at home and abroad and counts the trip to the Atlanta Olympics as the highlight of her involvement with Ian and the sport of horse trials.

Having owners who also understand racing and the costs involved has helped as Lord and Lady Hartington were used to the training fees and expenses involved, realising that it is the combination of good owners and sponsors that enables the team to keep going. Says Jenny: 'It costs about £10,000 to keep an advanced horse on the road and a big horse like The Moose is very expensive to run whereas Jack who so easily puts on weight, is on a permanent diet.'

Lady Hartington is a great supporter of the sport and the Stark entourage living the highs and lows so often experienced by many owners. 'In 1996 when Jack and Ian came so close to winning Badminton the tension was almost unbearable. Ian and Jack were less than one point behind the leader after the dressage and they managed to take the lead after their cross-country round. It was agony waiting in the collecting ring until it was Ian's turn and quite a lonely feeling. Jack jumped as well as he has ever done until he lost his concentration at the last two fences, which dropped them from first to sixth. The atmosphere was quite something and the gasp from the crowd was enormous, it was desperate to be so close.'

Nineteen ninety-seven was to prove a year of ups and downs for Lady Hartington's horses. After the excitement of leading following the dressage and cross-country at Badminton, she then put on a brave show when Jack hit five fences on the final day to drop to 13th place. Trotting up sound on the Monday after the trials, Jack was then taken for a routine check up at the Animal Health Trust at Newmarket where leg problems were diagnosed. Chairman of the senior selectors Giles Rowsell said the news was very sad, as Jack would definitely have been on the long list for the European Championships. But near the end of the season there was much to look forward to when Moose finished fifth at Blenheim, jumping one of only a handful of show-jumping clears.

Lady Hartington says that she gets a great deal of enjoyment from owning horses ridden by Ian from the fun that goes on behind the scenes to the excitement of the competition. 'Ian, Jenny, Tim and Stephanie make a great team, and however disastrously things turn out they have an amazing ability to bounce back. I really enjoy watching the young horses working their way up from Novice through to Intermediate to Advanced. I like watching Ian schooling, particularly doing the flat work. He is remarkable in that he seems to be able to mould any horse into shape. I have spent a lot of time walking courses with Ian and it is fascinating listening to his thoughts on how to approach and tackle each fence or combination as well as the gossipy tit-bits in between fences.

'Everyone is very friendly and ready to help each other in eventing, probably more so than in any other sport. I enjoy the hustle and bustle around the horse box and the tremendous adrenaline when the pressure is on. I like seeing the rosettes fluttering against the horses' heads, especially if they are red and of course I enjoy having the horses at home to ride and get to know while also learning about their personalities.

'The most unexpected things happen when you are with the Stark family. At the end of the 1997 season the grooms Sharon, Rachel and I went to Bishop Burton with Ian and Jenny. We had four horses on board belonging to various people and when we arrived there was fog swirling in and out. The organisers decided to start the competition but to delay the cross-country. It was a strange sight watching horses looming out of the fog and then disappearing again. It was almost impossible to see the horses at the other end of the dressage arena.

'As we were sitting in the horse box waiting for the fog to lift we were idly talking about the horses on board and what the future held for each of them. Ian mentioned that one was possibly for sale and I remembered that a friend of mine was looking for a hunter, and having looked on the map we realised she lived quite near. I then rang her to see if she was at home but she was out, searching for a horse that had thrown its rider whilst out hunting the day before and had galloped off into the fog.

'Meanwhile by mid day the fog had not lifted and by one o'clock the event had to be cancelled. I rang my friend again. She was back home having retrieved an unscathed horse six miles from where it had gone missing. She was still wanting a hunter for herself and asked if we would like to drop in for tea.

'We turned up to be greeted by a pot-bellied pig, anxious lest she was going to be upstaged by a newcomer to the menagerie. The horses were unloaded, my friend had a look at the one that was possibly for sale and as she liked the look of it Jenny and I frantically rang to find the owner and make sure it was indeed for sale. As Ian was showing the horse off, the pig snuffled around inquisitively, upsetting one of the horses who had never met such a curious creature before. To anyone looking on, we must have seemed a very odd bunch – horses, humans, dogs and one very busy pig, determined to get in on the act. As a result of this diversion Ian sold a horse to a very satisfied customer and a disgruntled pig called Angel.

'Another day I went to stay with the Starks before an event. I was hoping for an early night as we were leaving at 5.30 a.m. but no such luck! We spent the evening and most of the night dancing Scottish reels as the Stark family were celebrating in style. It was Jenny's sister's wedding. I did not have much style about me as I had come unprepared with clothes suitable only for an event, but no one seemed to mind and I was made to feel very welcome. Life with the Starks is never dull – I wish we were all ten years younger.

'The trip to Atlanta was a dream come true – you can't ask more than for your first event horse to be selected for the British team, an unbelievable honour. And apart from anything else, it was the best way of losing weight I have yet to discover! The trip was brilliantly organised by Patrick Beresford. We took out three children and a friend and travelled out with Jenny, Stephanie and Tim. We spent a week in a motel just across the road from the team. The build-up beforehand was thrilling. First on the long list, with sleepless nights worrying if Jack would be chosen for the short list. Then on the short list worrying about the intense heat and humidity in Atlanta – how badly would this affect him? Should we let him go out there?

'The competition itself was thrilling although we did not come home with a medal. All four horses in the team completed the event and we were placed fifth, quite an achievement but certainly not good enough for our critics. Jack and Ian did a brilliant dressage test, the best of any of the three-day event teams. Jack is also an excellent cross-country horse but this time it was not to be. He tripped in the first water and was unable to regain his balance before stumbling up the bank and then he tried bravely to jump the brush fence but it was impossible and he and Ian had a crashing fall.

'Watching it on the closed circuit television in the ten-minute box, I thought it was the end of the competition for them. Surely Ian or the horse was hurt but within moments they were both back on their feet and completed the course as if nothing had happened. Sadly this hiccup cost the team a lot of points and probably a medal. It was difficult to stomach. Ian and Jenny were brilliant with coping with such disappointment.

'After the competition was over my husband hired a mini-van and we all set off with the Stark family to a funfair to raise our spirits again. This didn't take long as there were huge rollercoasters and hair-raising bungee jumps. Tim and Stephanie have all the guts that their father has and off they went on every possible ride.'

Talking of her beloved Jack, Lady Hartington says: 'He is a great character, always interested in what everyone is doing and looking for fun. In Atlanta he crawled underneath the strap across his stable door and escaped, but instead of galloping round madly he took off for the nearest piece of grass and started eating which is quite typical. He is always looking for trouble and will do anything for Polos or sugar.

'Funnily enough Jack is more interested in showing off to people rather than horses and if he does start to mess about it is simply because he is being naughty and cheeky not nasty. He thoroughly enjoys being turned out during the winter and looks like a woolly pony when we bring him back into work in January. The only time he gets really cross is when he is back in full work and on a strict diet. Ever since Jack walked down the ramp of Ian's lorry he has been my favourite. He has such presence and a very cheeky face. He is extremely greedy and very inquisitive. His nose is like an elephant's trunk always questing in your pockets for tit-bits. When he is out at grass and I go to pull up any lurking shoots of ragwort he follows me around the field like a friend, watching with his ears pricked. Later in the year when I go to collect mushrooms he is equally intrigued and again follows me. One day he watched me until I had an armful of mushrooms and then nudged my elbow. As the mushrooms fell all over the ground he stood there looking at me. I could almost see him smiling, then he kicked his heels and trotted away. When he has his girth done up he invariably steps sideways as if wanting to step on your foot, and he has succeeded too many times for my liking.

'Another reason he means so much to me is because once we nearly lost him. One dark night flashes were seen from the kitchen window. They were in Jack's paddock. I screamed "Jack" and the rest of the family leapt to their feet and we rushed out to investigate. We saw the ground was alight with huge sparks shooting into the air and there was a loud roaring noise. The overhead mains high voltage cable had snapped and the live end had fallen to the ground causing the explosions, with a lethal current of 33,000 volts – enough to kill a crowd, let alone a horse. I could see nothing except this glaring light and then suddenly we heard galloping hooves and a lot of snorting and a ghostly figure flashed past, first one way and then back again, very close to the explosions. Most of the time we could only see his head because in those days his body was a lot darker and his white face stood out.

'Alex, our son-in-law, rushed to get the car to use the headlights, while our daughter Celina and I fetched buckets, nuts and ropes. To start with we could not get near him but luckily the rattle of nuts in a bucket helped to bring him to hand. He was trembling all over and dripping with sweat. Thank goodness he was safe. I stayed with him for most of the night. I could not believe that he was all right but the next day all seemed well – he had had a remarkable escape.

'Compared to Jack, Moose is a much more relaxing horse to be with. He is not an attention seeker! He stands at 18 hands and riding him is like sitting astride a marquee. Over the last two seasons he has improved with no fuss and has responded positively to Ian's work programme.

'As an owner I hope I offer the Stark team support and a bit of light relief

Ian's lorry showing the many sponsors who support the team

when things go wrong, although it is usually Jenny who holds us all together when things go wrong. She is the unsung heroine of the Stark team. Ian and I are fiercely competitive but luckily Jenny is not. She is the one who keeps a level head and smoothes out the wrinkles but really I am sure I get much more out of Team Stark than they do from me.'

. . .

Being involved with a number of firms on the sponsorship front, Bridgit Duerden has acted as Ian's unofficial agent since she first came into contact with him nine years ago. At the time Bridgit was working as marketing manager for equestrian wholesalers Westgate in Kent when she started to come across companies who were interested in getting involved with the eventing scene and a rider of Ian's calibre. Taking the pressure off Ian and Jenny who are always so busy, Bridgit liaises between the two parties to make sure everything runs smoothly.

Says Bridgit: 'I first met Ian when a firm wanted a celebrity to present a trailer to a prize winner and Ian made the presentation at Burghley. I was involved in a public relations role for the firm before going to work for Westgate.' Bridgit helped develop the relationship between Ian and 3M for Vetrap bandages, Super Solvitax the well-known equine health care brand of supplements, Eqvalan horse wormers and Aerborn rugs and accessories. The Vetrap contract came about when they were looking for a rider who was genuinely using the bandages as Ian was. All these companies help both financially and with supplying product as do Easyboot, Pittards Leather, Burgess Horse Feeds, Buckley Bits, Tippa Vacuum Systems and W.H. Malcolm Transport. It is a sign of Ian's standing in the eventing world and his effort to represent so many companies that he is involved with such a number of firms.

One of the highlights of Bridgit's association with Ian and Jenny was travelling out to Punchestown for the Europeans in 1991. Ian's win on Glenburnie led to a great deal of celebrating and as the championships were sponsored by Heineken the trophy was quickly filled with lager. Unable to finish it all Ian promptly tipped the contents over his head much to everyone's amusement. Later that evening, in an attempt to persuade the police to allow the bar to stay open, Ian was quickly recruited to sign their black books as the new European champion and the partying went on. Throughout her work with Ian, Bridgit says he has remained totally single-minded with a true winner's personality but what makes him so outstanding is his ability to get on with everyone and the time he has for people. 'Ian is a rider for the people and his fans are always assured his cross-country rounds will be thrilling. Nothing ever fazes Ian whether it is tackling a cross-country course or having a microphone pushed into his face. He rides like he drives and has always lived life to the full.

'I remember Ian holding a series of lecture demonstrations when the winner of a competition had the opportunity to ride Murphy. As soon as you put a child on his back he went very quiet and knew straight away not to tear about, but at one performance Ian was holding a lecture/demonstration for the Injured Jockeys Fund in Shropshire. Lord Oaksey was there and won the chance to ride Murphy which he decided to take up. Murphy immediately knew he had a man on board and took off round the arena. Ian and everyone who understood Murphy were left going whiter and whiter as he got faster and faster. The incident left Lord Oaksey totally unfazed but Ian was very relieved when he eventually managed to stop him.

Elaine Welsford took over from Bridgit at Westgate and continues to work closely with Ian and she says: 'The relationship has worked very well because people recognise that if Ian promotes a product and says it works it will. We know that if Ian tests a product for us it will be well tried, and his profile gives the product credence.

'Ian's biggest asset is his rapport with the general public and his ability to feel at ease in any company. We work with Ian at about six events every year including the BETA trade fair where he will come on the stand and talk about the products and we always know when Ian turns out for us Jenny will be there as well. Jenny is the engine room of the operation and gives as much help and support as Ian does.'

Super Solvitax, one of the brand leaders in equine feed supplements, has supported Ian for five years and now has a working relationship which benefits both Ian and the company. 'Ian is one of the greatest ambassadors for the company and for the sport that exists around the world,' says marketing manager Tony Day. 'He is synonymous with competitiveness and success and works hard to promote Super Solvitax. Sponsorship is a two-way process and we get a great deal from Ian.'

Aerborn Equestrian has also been closely linked to Ian providing rugs,

Ian and Stephanie in a publicity shot for sponsors Super Solvitax (Expo Life)

bandages and other equipment for the team. John McGowan the managing director had seen Ian competing at several events and was told he was looking for sponsors. At the time Aerborn was in the process of developing its new 'cushion web' range of girths, headcollars and lead reins. Aerborn knew that they had a good product line and wanted the endorsement of a top rider. Three-day eventing seemed like the right sport for the products and in particular the Aerborn girth as it would be tested in three disciplines. Knowing that Ian would not endorse a product without first testing, approving and liking it, a batch of girths was sent to him. He tried them for a period of time and came back saying they had worked very well and he would be more than happy to enter into a sponsorship agreement.

John McGowan says: 'From those early days, Ian has gone on to test and endorse other British made Aerborn products, safe in the knowledge that the company policy is to produce quality items which will stand the test of what is probably the most rigorous equestrian sport. Ian has appeared in Aerborn adverts, press releases and company brochures and his expertise in the care of horses during competition and at home has enabled him to offer advice to the company. He has also been instrumental in the improvement of existing products and development of new ones.

'Over the years Aerborn has organised a number of clinics and demonstrations with Ian. These have been all over the country with audiences of up to 1,500 people. They have given the public a chance to see Ian training his own and other peoples' horses, with the profit going to various equestrian related charities, in particular The Riding for the Disabled Association. The clinics have been a way of showing the close relationship between the Stark family and Aerborn and they have been good public relations for both parties.'

Burgess Supafeeds started to sponsor Ian in 1995 after he had tried the feed on his team of horses and liked the way they maintained condition. The company supply Ian with all his horse feeds, Supa Barley Rings and Supa Horse as well as keeping the dogs Lottie and Noodles in a good supply of their Supa Dog range of feeds. In return for this help Ian has carried out a number of talks to both the trade and consumer audiences. A special training day was organised for eight lucky winners from a magazine and an on pack promotion to have a lesson with Ian followed by a dressage and jumping demonstration for the winners and 100 runners-up was held.

To be involved with so many owners and sponsors is testament to Ian's standing within the sport and industry. It is because Ian is so willing to attend sponsors' days and events that they are willing to stay with him and their relationships grow and develop into much more than a business agreement.

10

The Trainers

'*Ian has received an enormous amount of help from Barbara Slane Fleming. He was always heading for the top but without help and instruction it would have been much more difficult to reach that level.*'

JENNY STARK

Throughout his career Ian has been connected to just a handful of trainers preferring to build up a good working relationship with them rather than move from one to another. These trainers include Barbara Slane Fleming, Ferdi Eilberg and Lars Sederholm, as well as Pat Burgess and Lady Hugh Russell from the early days of team training.

To achieve continued success in horse trials it takes hard work, dedication and a huge dose of natural talent. But to step from being a one-off wonder to becoming a household name for nearly 15 years is a remarkable achievement. Few top riders succeed without a strong back-up team of trainers, grooms and owners. And one trainer to have seen the many highs and lows of Ian's career is Barbara Slane Fleming, his dressage guru and mentor since the days of Oxford Blue and Sir Wattie. Now well into her 70s, Mrs Slane Fleming visits Ian at Haughhead occasionally to help with any problems and to watch the horses work.

Living just 50 miles away at Eglingham near Alnwick she is ideally located to make the short journey to Haughhead when it is time to look at the horses. Mrs Slane Fleming moved to the north more than 35 years ago, as she didn't enjoy the hunting in the south. Northumberland provided her with plenty of hunting and she has never considered going back to the south, much preferring the beautiful part of the country she has made her home and base.

Says Mrs Slane Fleming: 'I started helping Ian with Wattie when he was a five-year-old. Ian had come with Wattie and Oxford Blue on a course, I was running, and I told him he had two nice three-day event horses. After the course Ian tried one or two different trainers before he came back to me and we have worked together on the dressage ever since. He has been very loyal and I find him very easy to teach and he does what I say and produces the goods. Ian is very competitive. He appears so laid back and is always laughing, but deep down he very much wants to win and is very determined. His personality and way with people have made him a household name and he is so natural with the media, which has been a big help.'

From the beginning Ian struck Mrs Slane Fleming as a natural who just needed 'tidying up a bit'. 'At the early stage in his career he had never ridden an advanced dressage horse, so I put him on Whinbush, my main horse at the time and suggested we have a go at flying changes,' she laughs. 'It was interesting to say the least.'

Throughout their years as trainer and rider they have never seen each other constantly, simply keeping it to a few sessions in the spring followed by some help at the major three-day events. She has never travelled abroad to watch or help Ian as during team competitions a trainer is allocated to the squad.

A Fellow of the British Horse Society, Mrs Slane Fleming admits that horses have been her entire life since she started to ride on a donkey. On leaving Benenden School in Kent to pursue a career with horses she was told by her tutors it was a 'complete waste of time' and that she would 'never make it'. But make it she did and the knowledge she gained over the years has gone to making Ian so highly regarded in the dressage field, especially with Lady Hartington's elegant grey Stanwick Ghost.

Remembering some of the peaks of her relationship with the Starks, Mrs Slane Fleming says: 'Taking Wattie to Badminton for the first time when Ian was not really heard of was a real high. Then when he finished first and second on Wattie and Glenburnie in 1988 that was another moment that I will always remember.'

She says it was sad that Murphy Himself never won a championship with Ian and a tragedy that when lying in gold medal position at the Barcelona Olympics, Murphy trotted up lame. Mrs Slane Fleming will always have a soft spot for Murphy and feels he was the greatest horse Ian ever had, a free spirit who wouldn't be bossed about. 'Working with Murphy was always a challenge and you had to convince him what he was doing was right, rather than simply saying get on with it,' she says.

Of Ian's current team of horses she says she has always liked Stanwick Ghost from the very beginning especially as he was so much easier to train on the flat than both Murphy and Glenburnie. 'He thinks he is Desert Orchid, he is such a show-off at the trot-up and at Badminton last year just brought the house down at the final inspection. Lady Hartington's young pretender, The

Barbara Slane Fleming and Ian, Badminton 1997 (Tim Smith)

Moose, also shows great promise and, once he is more together and organised should be a top-class horse. Then of course there is Arakai, Lady Vestey's New Zealand thoroughbred who is absolutely fabulous. The display he showed round Badminton in 1997 was quite incredible. It was his first four-star event and proved Ian's faith in the horse.'

In the run-up to the 1997 season she concentrated on developing the flying changes, a new movement to the FEI test with Stanwick Ghost and Arakai. The sudden addition of flying changes to the dressage test had caused a huge amount of controversy. For the older, more established horses who were so used to executing counter canter, to suddenly ask them to carry out a flying change was at first very confusing. She feels the flying changes were introduced without enough warning and they have been put in the most difficult place for an event horse to execute the movement. 'As you come across the diagonal in big, medium canter strides you then have to bring the horse back to do a flying change. A dressage horse can do this easily by sitting back on its hocks to make the change, but an event horse is likely to be on the forehand.

'Stanwick Ghost, who is normally so trainable became very confused and felt if he changed he would be in trouble,' she explained. 'When we started to really put the pressure on him he became upset so we decided to leave him for a while and return to them later. Luckily this worked and once he understood what was wanted, the problems we had encountered disappeared.'

Having seen many horses come and go from Ian's yard, Mrs Slane Fleming is clear in her thoughts as to what makes a good event horse. 'Any decent cross-country horse must have some character and be slightly cheeky to be any good. If horses are too polite they will never make it round the cross-country where they have to think for themselves. It is no good horses always waiting to be told what to do on the cross-country, even though this is required for the dressage.'

After being involved with the family for so many years she has lived the roller-coaster of their life and says: 'There have been a lot of good times, they are quite simply, a super family.' At Badminton in 1997 she felt Ian had never ridden two cross-country rounds so well and once he had reached 40 she gave up telling him to retire, realising he wasn't going to take any notice. 'Ian has such a good team now, and as long as they are going well and staying sound I feel he will continue for a number of years. He hasn't had two such good horses as Stanwick Ghost and Arakai since Murphy and Glenburnie, and these two are definitely much easier.'

Specialising in training dressage riders, Mrs Slane Fleming has seen many of her pupils rise to the top and is glad that her knowledge, gained from many of the leading foreign trainers before the war, has been put to good use.

Knowing Ian so well, she concentrates her efforts on working the horse and has only had to correct Ian's position for a short period following a nasty fall at Charterhall some years ago which left him riding crooked, probably because of the severe pain he was in. At an event they will always follow a specific pattern, that they know works well and suits both. Ian will have one or two lessons that are nothing to do with the test to make sure the horse is working correctly and in the right frame of mind. From this they can establish how much time will be required to work-in for the test. Before a lesson Ian will have worked the horse to make sure it is sober and listening. Then before the test, Ian may only work the horses for ten to 15 minutes, with Mrs Slane Fleming giving small pieces of advice. 'I certainly don't start teaching them, before a test when it is far too late and better to leave Ian to his own thoughts.'

• • •

Another trainer to play an important role in Ian's success is Ferdi Eilberg, a well-known trainer and rider in the dressage world. He is responsible for helping many top riders on an individual front and for many years played a major role in assisting the British during team training and major championships as official trainer to the British three-day event team. Accompanying the team to European, World and Olympic championships, Ferdi helped the team to achieve much success in the dressage phase and has been influential throughout Ian's career.

'When I first moved to England from Germany,' says Ferdi, 'I worked with Richard Meade and became involved in team training in the early '80s. I first came into contact with Ian through team training before the Los Angeles Olympics when he was riding Oxford Blue and Sir Wattie. I remember he had just sprung into the limelight and Lorna Clarke who I was working with at the time said he was a name I would hear a lot more about.

'Like many people I thought Ian had come from nowhere and thought he

Ian on The Moose receives advice from Ferdi Eilberg (Tim Smith)

had a natural talent which could be developed. At that stage he was an efficient and capable rider in his own right and very good to work with because he would always be interested in what you were trying to do. If I told Ian to change how he was riding or gave him suggestions on what could be improved he always had a go and could put into practice what I was saying. During the team training sessions I would help Ian and his horses and worked quite a lot with Murphy and Glenburnie during their years together.

'Working with Ian and Murphy I was always conscious Ian had to work to bring the horse together more, if his movement became too big the transitions would not look quite so smooth and we always aimed for balance because his movement was always so impressive. Because both horses were so bold across country this sometimes made the dressage difficult and there was always a fine line when working with them about how much you could ask and persuade them to do.

'Having attended most of the major championships I have always watched Ian but after Barcelona in 1992, Chris Bartle started to help the team as I was getting more and more involved with riding in the dressage teams and the back-up squad was starting to change.'

· · ·

After encountering a number of problems with Stanwick Ghost's show-jumping Ian turned in 1996 to Lars Sederholm, a trainer of many well-known names. Ian felt his methods and ideas would be extremely beneficial and in the spring months before Badminton 1996 and 1997 he looked to Lars for help.

Swedish-born, Lars has been a teacher, trainer and coach to many top riders at his Waterstock training centre in Oxfordshire. A former member of the Swedish cavalry and then a groom for dressage rider Henri St Cyr, Lars moved to England in 1958 before moving to Waterstock in 1962 where his wife Diana's parents lived.

During training sessions he requires horse and rider to be very focused, the aim being to get both believing in themselves and that they are a success. Says Lars: 'Ian's horses had already benefited a great deal from his dressage work. In addition Ian has a natural eye for a stride and to start with two such healthy ingredients made the work with Ian very straightforward.

'The main work involved in connection with the flat work was recognising the difference between a show-jumping canter stride and a dressage canter. From a pure dressage point of view the higher the education level the less the horse uses his back in a suitable way for show-jumping. We therefore worked to increase the roundness of the canter stride. This was achieved by changing the horse's pace in canter with the rider alternating between sitting lightly on the horse and standing in the stirrups. The importance being that when the horse is collected the rider gets a sensation that the horse is very bold and brave with his back action. The horse should be able to canter so slowly that a person walking beside can keep up with him. All the time, however, when the change of pace is required, the horse's action and motivation should express itself to the fullest. We also wanted to recognise from which spot the different horses found it most comfortable to jump. The greatest horse in the world, Milton, was at his best, for example, when he left the ground from an early take-off, yet another horse might favour a closer take-off spot.

'When educating the horse in connection with jumping we worked so that the mechanism of the horse's canter stride could be compressed, but only to such an extent that the horse could handle this compression. Should the horse find this compression difficult he may twist or just hit the fence. Therefore the compression has to be worked on with an understanding for a gradual improvement. The natural jumper finds this easy but Jack did not.

'When a rider has an obedient horse, and the rider sees his stride well, it is only too easy for the rider to take over from the horse, especially if the horse is by nature not careful. In these circumstances the horses are inclined to listen more and more to the rider, and focus less and less on the obstacle. At home we experienced some very satisfying jumping but at a three-day event the horse and rider's technique is thoroughly tested after a fast cross-country performance. It is therefore of the utmost importance that the homework has been so established that the horse easily recognises the difference between the cross-country and the show-jumping. The not-so-careful jumper finds it difficult to switch from one to the other and often pays the penalty. Patience and repetition in the horse's homework have, from early on, to be the order of the day.

'During any training I use common sense. I try and get the horse to look after itself and once that has been achieved the rider can then start to play a part on how it performs, but the horse must think and use its brain. It is important to have continuous discussion and with Ian I talked extensively about the problems he was encountering so that I understood fully what was going wrong. Once I have listened to the various explanations and problems I can them make an assessment and we can work on putting right that problem. The rider and trainer must have complete trust and respect in each other and with all riders I like them to understand fully what we are trying to do. Unless the whole process is fully understood the rider cannot go and then use what he has learnt at a competition. I have had the great privilege of working with many talented riders, and Ian is one of the most gifted of all. That apart, it was a real pleasure to work with a true sportsman.'

'Jack's show-jumping is a handicap but thanks to Lars it did start to improve,' says Ian. 'As a novice he would think nothing of kicking out four or five fences and I have to confess we didn't spend too much time on show-jumping training in the past except at team concentrations and with some grid work at home in the school. I should have started going to Lars 20 years ago. There is so much to be learnt from him and he has a wonderful understanding of the horse's mind. The sessions I have spent with Lars have been very thought provoking and I always come away with a lot to think about.'

Schooling Sir Marcus at home (Expo Life)

11

Secrets of Success – Training

'I have a weird riding style. Probably this is because I learned on bareback ponies wearing headcollars. I don't know why I can't sit still a bit more. However much I work at sitting pretty at home, as soon as I am up against it my natural instinct takes over, trying to survive in the saddle.'

IAN STARK

Throughout his many years riding horses of all shapes, sizes and ability Ian has taken his own approach to schooling and training in the search for success instead of relying on text book principles. With the help of a handful of trainers he takes time to get to know a horse, how its brain works and what makes it tick in order to get the most out of it. If a horse requires more time to develop and mature it will be given that time and only when he is sure it is mentally and physically ready will he take it to a competition whether he is competing at novice or advanced level.

DRESSAGE

'When schooling at home I never do sessions which are very long. Obviously if I am going through a period when I'm trying to teach the horse a new movement or really establish the horse then I may have to work a little longer. And if we have hit a certain stumbling block or problem then I will keep going for as long as it takes,' explains Ian.

'This isn't always the answer though and when I was teaching Stanwick Ghost flying changes for the new movements in the test in the spring of 1997 we had quite a few problems. When I tried to keep going he just blew up and became impossible so the only option was to leave him. Suddenly after a break everything clicked, he knew what I wanted and relaxed. If we had kept pushing I don't think we would ever have got through and then you risk the possibility of the horse becoming very uptight when you try a movement because it remembers the bad experience.

'Years ago when I first had Wattie and he was about six I remember him being very naughty and not listening. We were using the indoor school and I wouldn't let anyone move for about three hours until I had won, but you have to weigh up every situation as it arises. Jenny was desperate to go to the loo and all I wanted to do was keep trotting a 20-metre circle to maintain Wattie's attention. It's never a case of being especially hard but the horse must understand what is wanted and if it means repeating the exercise a few times then that is the only answer until the horse is clear on what I expect.

'During a normal session schooling at home I spend about 20 minutes working the horse and always like them to have been hacked out before I start so they are settled and not too fresh. I never go out thinking I only have so much time with a horse because they get to know if you are riding to the clock and realise you have to stop at a certain point which is no good at all.'

Ian is a great believer in professional training and says that whatever a rider's standard it is always very useful to have someone with an 'expert eye' on the ground watching how the horse is working. Quite often a rider will feel his horse is working well but with a few words of advice from a trainer the horse's way of going can often be greatly improved. 'Whatever the standard of the horse, I feel it's very important to return to working on the horse's basic paces. Too often, when a horse has progressed to the stage of competing in a dressage test and started lateral work riders forget about the quality of the horse's movement. The aim of dressage training is to have the event horse obedient and moving in a soft, supple way,' says Ian. 'I like the horses to go forward freely in a correct rhythm and good balance. I would work a horse through all paces – walk, trot and canter – and make sure they are worked for equal periods on both reins so that the horse stays flexible throughout the whole body.

'When I take a horse into the school, I first allow them to settle down before the serious work begins. The aim is to get the horse to be long and low but staying round and maintaining impulsion – rather than stretching down, long and flat. This gives them a basis to work from and can be returned to if a horse becomes tense whilst working-in at a competition.'

'I do most of my schooling in rising trot, especially with the youngsters and only introduce sitting gradually when horses are strong enough in their backs and working correctly. Once basic trot and canter are established then I'd work the horses "forward and back" in trot and canter i.e. from working paces to lengthened strides, and, then back to working paces again and gradually as the horse progresses in his training, using collection as well, introducing lateral work when the rider feels the horse is physically and mentally ready. Varying the work keeps the animal interested and thinking. It is important to alleviate boredom as this can cause the horse to become inattentive and develop resistances.'

Once the horses are well into the Intermediate stage and nearly Advanced, Ian finds the everyday routine tends to fall very much into a pattern. Whilst all the horses have a forward plan, the work may be altered on a daily basis as required.

On the competition front and in the build-up to Badminton, Ian aims to compete at three one-day events with the horses. But, again there are exceptions with both Murphy and Glenburnie competing in just two before Badminton in order that they didn't get too excitable. All horses' temperaments are different and it is Ian and Jenny's experience of handling so many which tells them when a horse requires another outing while some may need to take a quieter competition route before the three-day events which are always the ultimate goal.

Ian is a great believer that competitions are won at home with a thorough preparation and training schedule. Whilst he trains and expects his horses to perform a test after 15 to 20 minutes working-in, he feels that if they are tense or excitable then lungeing or hacking them before their work can help. Sometimes, when a horse needs longer he prefers to work them for two or three short sessions rather than a solid one or two hours. 'The reason being that I think that horses relax better or more quickly and therefore work better than if they are out for too long a period when they start to go on nervous energy and show too much tension. The best work for the day has been and gone before the test!'

Ian's many years of experience at top-level eventing have given him a wealth of knowledge which he is always keen to pass on to younger riders who are equally keen to progress up the ladder. Many riders spoil their dressage tests by being inaccurate, in his view. But not every horse is blessed with wonderful conformation and paces, therefore the test should be accurate, obedient and with the horse working to the best of its physical ability; that must look pleasing and appealing to the judge.

SHOW-JUMPING

The show-jumping work carried out at Haughhead is a natural progression from the flat work. Grid work sessions are used to make the horses more careful and improve their technique. All jumping sessions start off with basic exercises on the flat to make the horse supple but making sure that the horse is always 'in front' of the rider's leg. What must be avoided is what some people think of as a dressage canter which is just slow and lacking impulsion, giving the horse no chance of jumping properly.

'Gymnastic work helps horses to learn the correct technique of rounding or basculing over a fence, using their neck and head and folding their legs up out of the way. As with dressage, some horses have more ability than others and all the jumping exercises should be designed to improve a horse's natural ability,' says Ian.

'The gymnastic grid work may also include one or more bounces to improve the horse's reactions, making them quick and neat. Balance is very important. Riders vary between the upright position and the forward seat. Both positions may need to be adopted depending on the horse you are riding – the aim being to remain in the middle of the horse allowing it freedom of movement.

'All work should also be done at home over related distances and riding turns. As the rider becomes more familiar with the horse's length of stride then it makes it easier for the rider to assess the striding to ride a course remembering that any alterations should be made early enough and not in the last one or two strides before a fence.

'How to ride the practice jumps at a competition again depends on the horse's ability and temperament. Most of my horses either trot or canter over a cross pole before jumping a few uprights, increasing in height then on to a spread fence, finishing with a relatively high, square parallel – providing the horse is remaining confident. Slightly careless horses may be better to go from a cross pole to a larger upright, omitting the steady increase in height as repetitive jumping of a single fence makes them stop trying for you. Out of preference I usually finish with an upright but the main thing is that at the final practice jump, the horse should feel as though he is concentrating, confident and trying to please.'

Practising over the show-jumps with Sir Marcus (Expo Life)

CROSS-COUNTRY

At home at Haughhead Ian has built a number of cross-country fences, which act as a good initial schooling ground for the horses. And, with a river running along the bottom of the fields, he is able to put this to good use for getting them used to jumping into water. In the case of younger horses Ian takes them to a variety of cross-country courses to practice, takes them hunting and team chasing before their first horse trials to make sure they are fully prepared and confident. Training is a time which allows riders to think about their approach to fences while rhythm, balance and speed are three of the main elements leading to a successful cross-country round within the time.

'Rhythm and careful course walking are the important factor on the cross-country course which get competitors round within the time. It was sometimes more difficult to finish inside the time on strong fast horses like Murphy and Glenburnie, than it was with Wattie who never had their speed but who never needed checking on the approach to a fence so I could keep at a constant pace. Many of the top riders appear to be travelling very slowly on the cross-country when in fact they are using the terrain and cutting off valuable seconds by their approach to a fence.

'It is important that you walk the course thoroughly beforehand and have everything clear in your mind before you set out. For many riders, including myself, it is the thrill of the cross-country that is the motivation behind competing in eventing.

'Walking the course is an essential part of the whole competition giving the riders the opportunity to familiarise themselves with the fences, the course in general, the ground and where time can be saved. At a three-day event I would normally walk the course at least three times. The first walk is to get a general impression and view of the course, to see what the fences are like and where each one is going. The second walk is to look at all the alternatives and the final walk is to decide exactly which routes to take.

'It is important to remember the horse never gets the opportunity to see the fences and course until it is galloping round it and success is often down to the rider understanding their horse, knowing how it will cope with certain ground and what fences it may be unsure about.

'At a one-day event I only have the time to walk the course once and have to assess quickly which route I will take. My choice is nearly always to go the

Sir Marcus clears a cross-country fence at Haughhead (Expo Life)

quick route but this depends on the horse's experience and the ground conditions. Whenever I walk a course I always go through the start and finish then at least I think I may have a chance of going through them on the day.

'At top-level competition riders all wear stop-watches for the speed and endurance phase as the time factor is so critical. But, at novice level I believe riders should go round without a watch so they get used to riding according to how the horse feels and learn to ride in a rhythm. The more riding you do, the more you develop a feel for the correct pace.

'Everyone has their own way of coping in the ten-minute box at a three-day event but you must start by entering the area in a sensible state of mind and if the horse is excitable it is better to walk or trot quietly before the box. The heart rate is important and I like to walk the horse for a while before arriving there. I prefer not to take the saddle off but do slacken the girth and undo the noseband so the horse can relax a little. After washing the horse down and checking shoes and studs I allow myself four minutes to tighten the girth and noseband and apply grease to the horse's legs on the stifles, joints and forearms but not the chest as this stops the horse from sweating. Once on board (Jenny usually gives me a leg on), I get the soles of my boots wiped to make sure they are dry and clean, so there's less chance of my feet sliding out of the stirrups!'

BITTING

When it comes to bitting a horse, Ian tries to keep everything simple, preferring snaffles. If the horse is light-mouthed he might use a nathe bit or, if he leans, then he would have a 'French link' but nearly always use these bits with cheek pieces. Although he has had some very strong horses and used much stronger bits, he thinks horses should always be given the benefit of the doubt and started in milder bits, remembering that safety of horse and rider is paramount so one should always be in control.

Whatever bit is used must be the right size for the horse's mouth and correctly fitted. Even a badly fitting snaffle can cause pain and discomfort and horses always run from pain. Ian has changed bits on horses that have come to him because every partnership with a bit is different and what suits one rider will probably not suit another and he recalls: 'When I had Murphy he was very strong and it took us a while to sort out his brakes. In his case a stronger bit was not the only answer to his strength across-country. We did eventually find that an American cherry roller gag with a combination noseband suited him. I spent a whole spring season with Murphy going very slowly round courses in a steady canter not allowing him to get overexcited and gallop. This theory worked until the steeplechase at Badminton when Murphy remembered where he was and went into overdrive.'

Ian is much in demand as a teacher and here demonstrates the correct jumping position
(Tim Smith)

Postscript

AND TO THE FUTURE . . .?

During nearly 26 years competing in horse trials all over the world Ian has given countless lecture/demonstrations which never cease to prove hugely popular and a big success. Such events give his army of fans and followers, both old and new, an exclusive insight into his training methods, hectic lifestyle and personality, allowing them to gain the answers to the many questions they have longed to ask.

In the early months of 1997 Ian was asked to present a lecture/demonstration at Patchett's Equestrian Centre in Hertfordshire. He took his top four horses for the season Stanwick Ghost, Arakai, The Moose and Sir Marcus. The large number of people who had turned out to watch that evening saw each horse worked through the different stages in their training both on the flat and over jumps, and few watching that night could fail to be impressed by the natural talent and dedication for which Ian has become known. His natural ability as an all-round horseman had conjured up a magical evening for spectators giving them a brief insight into his methods, theories, philosophies and character. The applause that he received at the end as well as a non-stop flow of questions proved The Stark Approach was as popular as ever.

There can be few people involved in eventing who have never stopped to think just what it is that makes top riders like Ian want to continue year upon year, striving to maintain their position at the top of the sport. Is it the money, the fame, the glory, the thrill of the cross-country or the fact they have become a household name? Or is it their love of the horse and the partnership that must evolve for the ultimate goal of winning to be achieved?

Looking to the future and with the Sydney Olympics taking place in the year 2000 Ian is already working towards his next big challenge and with a top-class team of horses in the yard at Haughhead he is years away from hanging up his boots.

As the 1998 season approached Ian's team was headed by Lord and Lady Vestey's hugely talented New Zealand thoroughbred Arakai, who was aimed at Badminton along with Lady Hartington's The Moose who was rapidly gaining experience. These two were backed by new arrivals Jaybee and Saucy Brown for Lady Hartington while the much loved Stanwick Ghost, out of action for much of 1997, looked set to return to the scene in the autumn, giving Ian a stable full of stars to keep him at the top . . .

The current campaigners: (left to right) *The Moose, Saucy Brown, Jaybee, Arakai* (Peer Ahnert)

Major Awards

1983
1st Bramham, Sir Wattie, 3rd Oxford Blue
2nd Achselschwang (Germany), Sir Wattie – winning team
7th Boekelo (Holland), Oxford Blue – winning team

1984
3rd Badminton, Oxford Blue
6th Badminton, Sir Wattie
1st Bramham, Charlie Brown IV
9th and team silver Olympic Games, Los Angeles, Oxford Blue

1985
1st Bramham, Deansland
Individual bronze and team gold, European Championships, Burghley, Oxford
Blue

1986
1st Badminton, Sir Wattie
11th and team gold, World Championships, Gawler, Australia, Oxford Blue
Individual bronze and team gold, Senior European Championships, Bialy Bor
(Poland), Sir Wattie
4th Burghley, Glenburnie
4th Le Touquet (France), Glenburnie

1987
Badminton cancelled
Individual silver and team gold, European Championships, Luhmuhlen (Germany), Sir Wattie

1988
1st Badminton, Sir Wattie
2nd Badminton, Glenburnie
2nd and team silver, Olympic Games, Seoul, Sir Wattie
1st Boekelo (Holland), Murphy Himself
1st Windsor, Mix N' Match

1989
1st Osberton, Washington II
4th Badminton, Glenburnie
5th Badminton, Murphy Himself
8th and team gold, European Championships, Burghley, Glenburnie

1990
14th Badminton, Murphy Himself
15th Badminton, Glenburnie
Individual and team silver, World Equestrian Games, Stockholm, Murphy Himself

1991
2nd Badminton, Murphy Himself
6th Badminton, Glenburnie
8th Bramham, Skean Dhu
6th British Open Championships, Gatcombe Park, Murphy Himself
Individual and team gold, European Championships, Punchestown, Ireland, Glenburnie

1992

5th Windsor, Clan Royal
4th Blair Castle, Stanwick Ghost
Olympic team member, Barcelona, Murphy Himself

1993

2nd Saumur (France), Stanwick Ghost
8th Punchestown (Ireland), Clan Royal
3rd Windsor, Dear Hardy
4th Blenheim, Stanwick Ghost

1994

8th Punchestown (Ireland), Stanwick Ghost
11th Burghley, Caliber
2nd Bramham, Kilcoran

1995

6th Saumur (France), Mr Mackinnon
10th Badminton, Caliber
4th Chantilly (France), Sir Marcus
9th Burghley, Mr Mackinnon

1996

6th Badminton, Stanwick Ghost
1st Bramham, Forest Glen
5th Olympic Games, Atlanta, USA, team competition, Stanwick Ghost
8th Burghley, Forest Glen
9th Le Lion D'Angers (France), The Moose

1997

13th Badminton, Stanwick Ghost
14th Badminton, Arakai
5th Blenheim, Moose
Team gold, Open European Championships, Burghley, Arakai